GOING FORTH IN THE NAME

Dear "Sister"

May you always know the love and peace that only Jesus can give.
(John 14:27)

Thanks for all your help in the past, as well as the days ahead.

Glenn

GOING FORTH IN THE NAME

The RVer' s Guide to
Living the Christian Life

Glenn Rivers

To order additional copies of this book, contact:
Xlibris Corporation
1-888-795-4274
www.Xlibris.com
Orders@Xlibris.com
56575

This book is dedicated to the Lord Jesus Christ; to the members of the Adventureland Congregation, past and present; and to my longtime friend Mr. Charles Ziehl. Without the help and encouragement from all of these, this book simply would not have been written.

> I can do all things through Christ who strengthens me.
> —Philippians 4:13 (NKJV)

A special thank-you to Sandi for rearranging her life so that the writing process could go forward!

CONTENTS

CHAPTER 1

A New Phenomenon

Dear friend, you are faithful in what you are doing for the brothers, even though they are strangers to you. They have told the church about your love. You will do well to send them on their way in a manner worthy of God. It was for the sake of the Name that they went out.

—3 John:5-7 (NIV)

IN THE ABOVE passage, the apostle John is commending his friend Gaius for graciously receiving and showing hospitality to a group of travelers, which the text simply refers to as "brothers." The word we translate "brothers" or "brethren" (KJV) was used in the New Testament to refer generically to fellow Christians of both genders, and he could easily have been referring to "brothers and sisters." John really does not say specifically who these "brothers" were or what their function was. We only know for sure that they were Christians and that they were traveling "for the sake of the Name" when they met Gaius and he showed them hospitality "in a manner worthy of God."

What impressed me when I read this passage of scripture and selected it as the basis for the title of this book is that there were these people in that biblical setting who were traveling for the Lord Jesus. John says, "It was for the sake of the Name [of Jesus Christ] that they went out." We know that we who are Christians are called upon by our Lord to do everything we do "for the sake of the Name."

Twenty-first Century Travelers

For more than a decade I have been part of a group of people who are known as "full-time RVers." We all live exclusively in our motor homes or trailers and travel all over the country. There are also some that I call "part-time RVers" who have a home or home base where they live part of the year, and they travel in their RVs for the remainder of the year. There are many of us among this number who are believers in Jesus Christ. If we bear the name "Christian," we should be making it our goal and purpose to be led by God's Holy Spirit and to go forth in our travels "for the sake of the Name."

This book is about more than just going to church. It is about more than having a devotional life. It is about more than practicing Christian ethics. *Christianity is a relationship with the living Jesus Christ.* It is not really about where and when you go to church and how often. It is not about whether you "cuss, smoke, drink, or chew"; it is about a real, living, one-on-one relationship with the Lord of the universe, and about how to draw closer to Him and live a life pleasing to Him while you are pursuing the RV lifestyle. This is the central idea that I wish to talk about in this book.

Moreover, if you do not have this personal relationship with Jesus Christ, the things we will talk about in these pages will be meaningless to you. The apostle Paul reminds us,

> The man without the Spirit does not accept the things that come from the Spirit of God, for they are foolishness to him, and he cannot understand them, because they are spiritually discerned. (1 Corinthians 2:14, NIV)

Only after we are "born of the Spirit" (John 3:6) can we understand those things that only the Holy Spirit can teach us.

I would be remiss if I did not say from the very beginning that in order to call yourself a "Christian," you need to have this one-on-one relationship with Jesus Christ Himself. It needs to be *your* faith and *your* relationship with Him, by His grace, through your faith (Ephesians 2:8).

Many of us will be fortunate in that we are able to identify a moment that we established that all-important relationship with Jesus Christ. To others it will seem more of a gradual thing. Some of you who were fortunate enough to grow up in dedicated Christian homes will possibly have a sense of the Lord always being near and being a part of your life. There may be different experiences, but it is the same reality. The "common denominator" will be our Lord Jesus Christ. The apostle John tells us at the very beginning of his Gospel,

> Yet to all who received him, to those who believed in his name, he gave the right to become children of God. (John 1:12, NIV)

The simple act of receiving Him is the start of this great adventure that we call "the Christian Life."

When Is Your Spiritual Birthday?

I know people who struggle with this whole issue as to when their "spiritual birthday" was. Many cannot identify a day, either by date or by recollection, that this occurred for them. Others have had more than one event in which Christ manifested Himself in their life, and they are uncertain at which of these events they were "saved."

The Bible promises us,

If you confess with your mouth that Jesus is Lord and believe in your heart that God raised him from the dead, you will be saved. (Romans 10:9, NLT)

It does not say that you will be a full-grown Christian immediately, and I think that this is part of the problem. Many do not understand how they can wander away from Christ as they sometimes do and can still belong to Him.

Many see salvation as an event. Others see it as a process. At the risk of sounding trite, I believe that salvation is, at once, both an event and a process and that the two are inseparable. As Paul shared the Lord's promise with the Philippians and with us,

I am sure that God, who began the good work within you, will continue his work until it is finally finished on that day when Christ Jesus comes back again. (Philippians 1:6, NLT)

Note that this passage says that God began our salvation, and it is He who will bring it to its completion. Saving people is *God's* business. The scriptures give us this further assurance:

No one is able to say, "Jesus is Lord," except by the Holy Spirit. (1Corinthians 12:3, NLT)

I do not think it is particularly important that you know what *day* it all began. What is important is that we know that we have a relationship with Jesus Christ. The next most important thing is that the relationship continues to grow. Aside from a person being lost without Christ, I believe that there is nothing sadder than a Christian who does not grow.

If you know that you have established this all-important relationship with Him, just sit back and enjoy the ride in your journey to get closer to Him and to walk daily with Him. If you have doubts about your relationship with Christ, then, by all means, examine your heart as you read these pages and settle it with Him once and for all. If you ask Him, He will not turn you away.

> For the same Lord over all is rich to all who call upon Him. For "whoever calls on the name of the Lord shall be saved." (Romans 10:12-13, NKJV)

My own "spiritual birthday," the beginning of my relationship with Jesus Christ began when I was twelve years old. I had a spiritual and what I choose to call a "redemptive encounter" with the Lord. There were no bright lights or audible voices, just the strong and comforting assurance as I asked the Lord to come into my life that He loved me and was going to be with me always. I knew little about the Bible at this time, and this spiritual experience was far from what I expected to happen. While I make this sound like something ethereal and "otherworldly," it was not that at all, but was something very real. In fact, I felt as though I was in touch with the Ultimate Reality. By the time this writing is published, it will have been over fifty years since that night, but that encounter was so profound and so real that it has sustained me through the ups and downs of the intervening half century.

It is significant to me that this encounter did not occur in a church, although I was highly influenced by what I had been hearing in the small country church where my dad's oldest brother was an active member and a deacon. I had been visiting my uncle's farm for a time that summer. My "redemptive encounter" occurred several hours after we had come home from church one Sunday evening as I pondered the things I had been hearing from the scriptures and as I prayed alone in my room after bedtime that night. Beyond the significance of the event itself, I certainly began to realize at this point that "the Lord does not dwell in houses made with hands" (Acts 7:48), but can be encountered anywhere in His creation. While this is one of those self-evident truths, it is one that many of us have a hard time conceptualizing.

I don't want to dwell too much on the period of the next thirty-nine years, as they have little to do with being a full-time RVer. So let's fast-forward to 1997.

This whole experience of drawing closer to the Lord while being a full-time RVer has been a pilgrimage for me. I refer to the period of about 1980-2001 as my "wandering period." I had wandered away and grown distant from Him during this time. I can also see, as I have looked back, that He went into the wilderness to seek the sheep that was straying (Matthew 18:12).

By the time 1997 rolled around, I had been retired from my twenty-five-year career in law enforcement for about a year and a half. We had just finished selling our house and "downsizing" our life so that we could become full-time RVers, a dream for which we had been planning for over a decade.

At this time in my life, I would definitely have to say that I had gotten away from the Lord. I hadn't attended church regularly since 1989. I usually managed to attend at Christmas and Easter, and maybe if someone invited us to their church for some special reason, but that was about it.

Personal Bible reading and prayer were even more sporadic in my life than church attendance. Most of the vestiges of the Christian lifestyle I had once lived had become dormant, to say the least. I had certainly retained my integrity. The memory of the power of God working in my life, particularly during my college years, was still vivid. But the life I had lived among the fellowship of believers was, to my way of thinking at that time, a thing of the past.

I had a general sense of "rightness" about the direction my life was going at this time, but I started to feel that God was trying to get my attention and that He should be a greater part of my life than I was allowing Him to be.

I had been listening to a lot of motivational speakers during those years. As you may know, a major theme among motivational speakers is that of goal setting. This was one of the good habits I had picked up from listening to them. Several of them had suggested that it might be a good idea to have goals for several areas of one's life. Some even suggested that one's goals should include some "spiritual" goals. I remember that during that first few years on the road, I set a "spiritual" goal to attend church five times. That sounds easy enough, right? I distinctly remember that I failed to make that goal the year I set it! I think at that point I realized how difficult it was to attend church in strange places when you are out on the road.

Another spiritual goal that I set for myself back then was to begin reading the Bible again. I had once been an avid student (and sometimes even teacher) of the Bible, so I exhumed my favorite study Bible from storage, dusted it off, and set a goal for myself to read a chapter a day. This goal I found much easier to achieve, and I found myself being blessed as I read God's word each day. As I look back, this was probably the single most influential thing that I did to get myself moving on the path back to God's way.

As time went on, I began to sense that God was speaking to my heart about returning to the fellowship of believers. By 2001 we had become "Workampers" and were beginning our fourth season working at Adventureland.[1] The park had started an employee worship service the previous year. My wife, Sandi, had attended the previous season, but I had not. Having been encouraged by some of the others and having had one of my major excuses removed, I too began attending the Adventureland congregation the next year. I really didn't expect too much. I had been to this sort of thing throughout the years, and I thought it would just be a bunch of folks "playing church" and trying to assuage their guilt for not attending "real church." Was I ever wrong about that! What I found was a dynamic group of folks that loved one another and loved the Lord and loved to sing His praises and hear His word preached. It was even more meaningful to me since my work at Adventureland had increasingly become the center of my life. Now I began to see that Jesus Christ was an evident part of Adventureland too!

Through my experience in the Adventureland congregation, God began to revive my heart. Singing new songs of praise and hearing faithful men of God (mostly local pastors and other Christian ministers) proclaim His word reminded me once again that Jesus Christ was alive! I could see that not only was the Holy Spirit actively at work in the world, but that He wanted to be active in *my life* each and every hour of each and every day.

Over the course of the next few years, I began to spend time daily with Him in prayer, and I once again became an avid student of His word. We found a new "home church" (in our designated hometown), and I became a Gideon. We have also become much more zealous to find a church to attend wherever we travel.

It was also at this time that I began to notice how many Christians there were, not only there at Adventureland, but everywhere I went in my RV travels. After being on the road for over a decade, I can truthfully say that I know more believers both on and off the road than I have at any time before in my life. I have come to believe that there is something more going on out here than just the fact that there are some Christians who are full-timers. I have come to believe that God is calling us out and placing us out here on the road. There is this large community of full-timers out here, and I believe that He is calling us to be salt and light among them. Also, there are a large number of missionary opportunities available to us as well. This is a need we could never fill if we remained "planted" in our home churches.

There are probably many reading this, and living the full-time RV lifestyle, to whom God is speaking about making the transition from "going forth" to "going forth in the Name." Everywhere I look, I see evidence that God is at work among RVers, both calling people unto Himself and calling His people back to Himself, as He did me.

In our Bible study group at Adventureland one past summer (of which, out of the fifty to sixty participants, about 90 percent are full-timers), we discussed how that among our RVing peers, most of those in the age group that is represented have attended a church or had some exposure to the Gospel. There are many who need to come to know the Lord personally for the first time. There are others whose hearts need to be renewed once again. Everywhere across this land, hearts are in need of the changes that only Jesus Christ can make.

There are many also who are using the RV lifestyle, either consciously or subconsciously, to "hide from God"; and like Jonah of old, they think that they can avoid following him by avoiding contact with the fellowship of believers. Well, friends, "you can run but you can't hide." The Hound of Heaven is hunting you down as we speak, and He is using the efforts of those of us who are going forth in His Name to get the job done for Him. Listen to His voice as He calls to you out on the road.

A Life on the Road

The comparison of today's Christian full-time RV travelers and the traveling brethren in the above passage in John is a general one, to say the least. While we read about a lot of traveling going on in the New Testament, particularly in the book of Acts, we can hardly compare the kind of traveling that they did with today's full-time RVers. The full-time lifestyle is a new social phenomenon unique to twentieth—and twenty-first-century America. The travelers in the book of Acts, and elsewhere in the New Testament, probably would have been just as content to stay put in familiar communities; but the economic upheaval and social unrest of their day, and particularly the persecution of the Christian church, served as an impetus that moved them around the Roman Empire. In our time, RV travel is an outgrowth of modern technology, economic prosperity, and social and political freedom unprecedented in the history of the world.

In our day, we are traveling for the sheer pleasure of it all. Even $3-plus-a-gallon gas prices have barely slowed us down from our desire to see the world and to experience the freedom of the road. Traveling in our RV homes gives us a dimension of traveling experience that is often hard for our non-RV friends and family to understand.

How many full-time RVers are there? No one really knows for sure. I have heard estimates as high as a half-million and would not be surprised to hear credible guesses as high as 1 or even 2 million. Why, in a country of 300 million occupants, could there not be as many as 1 or 2 percent who are full-timers?

As we have said, in the first-century church, there was a lot of movement going on. One has only to read the book of Acts to see a community of believers that God purposely scattered to the four winds so that His message of redemption in Jesus Christ could be carried to the known world of that day, and eventually to every nation on the earth. Indeed, the book of Acts is going to be somewhat of a scriptural model for us as we consider how to live the Christian life as we travel the highways and byways of our world.

Being a full-time RVer presents us with some unique challenges to living the Christian life. In the pages ahead, we will discuss these challenges. Much of what I will talk about will be my own experiences. Much more will be about how things *ought* to be, rather than how they *really* are in my life. I can think of many among my own acquaintances who seem more qualified than myself to talk about what it means to stay close to the Lord on the road. Yet as the scriptures tell us, God has chosen the weak things of the world (1 Corinthians 1:27) to carry His message, and this is the burden He has put on my heart. I do not present myself or my experience as the shining example of the things we will discuss. I present myself only as a fellow pilgrim on this journey with the Lord Jesus. Join me now as we look at how to confront these unique challenges of following Him down this both real and metaphoric "road."

CHAPTER 2

"Following the Son": A Life in the Spirit

For all who are led by the Spirit of God are children of God.

—Romans 8:14 (NLT)

B EING A FULL-TIME RVer is often referred to as "following the sun." Some Christian friends of mine have adapted this phrase on their calling cards to read, "Following the Son." I don't think this adaptation is original to them, but it truly captures in a single phrase what being a Christian RVer is all about.

It must be understood that living the Christian life, whether you are a full-time RVer or not, is, in its proper form, a life that is lived by following the Holy Spirit of God. I will have a lot more to say about that at various points along the path of this discussion, but we need to remember the words of the apostle Paul:

> Since we are living by the Spirit, let us follow the Spirit's leading
> in every part of our lives. (Galatians 5:25, NLT)

A New Look at an Old Truth

I have always had a great deal of interest in church history. I am particularly interested in the first two centuries: the time of Jesus and the apostles and the century immediately following their earthly lifetimes. We in the Evangelical tradition tend to look up to those early Christians, particularly those in the book of Acts, and throughout the first century. We often like to think of ourselves as the "New Testament Church." We look to the writings of the New Testament to give us our information about the things that we are to believe and how we are to conduct our lives. They also provide us with a model for our churches. Many Evangelical churches try to emulate the New Testament model(s) of church government and structure.

As I took a fresh look at the New Testament Christians when I began to write this book, I realized a truth, which at some level I guess I had always known; but for the first time, I was struck by its implications. It was a truth that "blew me away." That truth was the realization that the members of the New Testament Church *did not have Bibles available to them for everyday use!*

Now, I don't know about you, but I simply cannot imagine trying to live the Christian life without a Bible at my fingertips! I am one of these people who are always asking, "what does the Bible say" about this or that? You will notice, if you have not already, that I often try to make a point by quoting a passage of scripture and telling you what "the Bible says" about something. Yet these esteemed first-century believers did not have this advantage. Indeed, until the later part of that first century, most of our all-important New Testament had not yet been completely written, much less circulated to *all* the churches. How then did these early believers, whom we hold in such high esteem, manage to live the Christian life without regular and consistent access to a Bible?

It is true that the Old Testament existed at that time in what was, to them, a "modern" translation.[2] However, books were very hard to come by and very expensive. Probably many of the churches, especially those that started in synagogues, had copies of the Old Testament that they used in worship services and for other purposes in the church, but these would have been too scarce and expensive for most people to have in their homes. Obviously, carrying scriptures around with them, tucked beneath their arms or in their pockets, would have been completely out of the question!

And then there was the literacy factor. The percentage of people who could read in that day was comparatively small. The apostle Paul obviously had committed much of the Old Testament scriptures to memory. Probably he was not alone in this practice. The average New Testament Christian, however, particularly those who were Gentile believers, had only a very limited knowledge of, and access to, the scriptures.

How then did these New Testament era believers get by without the Bible tucked under their arms everywhere they went? What did they use as a guide to living the Christian life? *They lived by the guidance of the Holy Spirit of God!*

The book of Acts is full of statements like "being sent out by the Holy Spirit" (13:4), "they were forbidden by the Holy Spirit" (16:6), and so on.

The contexts of the two verses cited in the beginning of this chapter are classic examples of Paul's teaching about the Holy Spirit and the life of the Christian in the Spirit. The reader would do well at this point to stop and read the fifth chapter of Galatians and the eighth chapter of Romans to understand a summary of Paul's teaching on the Holy Spirit. These passages very clearly set out a comparison of the differences between following the desires of the sinful nature in us all and the nearly opposite concept of following the Spirit of God.

The whole of the New Testament is packed with references to the Christian life as being a life of following the Spirit of God who is within us. And the Old Testament is not without direct references to the Holy Spirit, as well as an abundance of indirect allusions to Him and His work among God's people.

Probably the best and most complete discussion of the Holy Spirit comes from Jesus Himself. After all, it is Himself of whom He speaks. John records Jesus' discourse to His disciples in the fourteenth, fifteenth, and the sixteenth chapters of his Gospel. I invite you to read these three chapters before we take a look at selected verses that are of primary interest to us.

First, Jesus introduces us to the Holy Spirit:

I will ask the Father, and he will give you another Counselor to be with you forever—the Spirit of truth. The world cannot accept him, because it neither sees him nor knows him. But you know him, for he lives with you and will be in you. I will not leave you as orphans; I will come to you. Before long, the world will not see me anymore, but you will see me. Because I live, you also will live. (John 14: 16-19, NIV)

The word that we translate in English "counselor," or in some translations "advocate" or "helper," means "the one who walks beside us to help us."[3] Jesus calls Him "the Spirit of truth." He is unknown and unseen to a lost world, but believers know Him because He is with us and in us, and we interact with Him regularly. Jesus here promises us that we will not be as orphans in this world as we sometimes think and act but that our Father will be with us, and He will be with us in the form of the Holy Spirit. We will "see" Jesus through the work and presence of the Holy Spirit because Jesus is alive, and by His Spirit, we too will be truly alive in this world.

Jesus goes on to say,

Whoever has my commands and obeys them, he is the one who loves me. He who loves me will be loved by my Father, and I too will love him and show myself to him. (14:21, NIV)

Jesus here tells us He will love us and show Himself to us. Remember now that this is just a few hours before the beginning of His trial and death on the cross. How will He show Himself to those who love Him if He is going to be taken from this world in just a few moments? By His Holy Spirit.

Then He says,

> All this I have spoken while still with you. But the Counselor, the Holy Spirit, whom the Father will send in my name, will teach you all things and will remind you of everything I have said to you. (14:25-26, NIV)

Have you ever been reminded by the Holy Spirit of a passage of scripture that speaks to your need of the moment? Most of us who have spent time in the word have had frequent occurrences of this experience.

> I am the vine; you are the branches. If a man remains in me and I in him, he will bear much fruit; apart from me you can do nothing. If anyone does not remain in me, he is like a branch that is thrown away and withers; such branches are picked up, thrown into the fire and burned. If you remain in me and my words remain in you, ask whatever you wish, and it will be given you. This is to my Father's glory, that you bear much fruit, showing yourselves to be my disciples. (John 15: 5-8, NIV)

Here again Jesus talks to us about abiding in Him as though it will be a future event, even though He knows and tells the disciples that His death is just moments away. He is talking about their future. They are to abide in Him because He will be with them always, wherever they may go, through the presence of His Holy Spirit.

> When the Counselor comes, whom I will send to you from the Father, the Spirit of truth who goes out from the Father, he will testify about me. (16:26, NIV)

In addition to the fact that the Spirit will testify about Jesus, He tells us in this passage that the Spirit is sent from, and goes out from, the Father.

Years later, John will say it this way when he writes to the churches who would receive his Epistle:

> And it is the Spirit who testifies, because the Spirit is the truth.
> (1 John 5:6, NIV)

Even though a period of over a half century had passed since Jesus had uttered the words about the testimony of the Spirit to the truth of the Gospel, John was still, in this pastoral letter, reminding his people of this marvelous truth.

> Finally, in His teachings about the Holy Spirit during His farewell address, Jesus says,
>
> But I tell you the truth: It is for your good that I am going away. Unless I go away, the Counselor will not come to you; but if I go, I will send him to you. When he comes, he will convict the world of guilt in regard to sin and righteousness and judgment: in regard to sin, because men do not believe in me; in regard to righteousness, because I am going to the Father, where you can see me no longer; and in regard to judgment, because the prince of this world now stands condemned.
>
> I have much more to say to you, more than you can now bear. But when he, the Spirit of truth, comes, he will guide you into all truth. He will not speak on his own; he will speak only what he hears, and he will tell you what is yet to come. He will bring glory to me by taking from what is mine and making it known to you. All that belongs to the Father is mine. That is why I said the Spirit will take from what is mine and make it known to you. (16: 7-15, NIV)

Here He is telling us, first of all, that the coming of the Holy Spirit will remove the geographic limitations imposed by Jesus' being in the flesh and therefore only able to be in one place at a time. The idea that God is everywhere and sees everything was about to take a new twist. He would now be "up close and personal" through the intimate work of the Holy Spirit in every believer.

Although the disciples didn't yet know it, the Christian faith was poised to become a spiritual force that would go into the entire world, both the known world of that day and the entire world as we know it now. The disciples had been in Jesus' presence nearly constantly for the last three years. Even though it was now time for Him to leave this earth and return to the Father, this situation of being in the presence of Jesus would continue because of the presence of His Holy Spirit in them.

Jesus said that the presence of the Holy Spirit would bring conviction into the world, conviction of sin and of righteousness and of judgment. When we say we are "convicted" or "under conviction" for our sin, it is more than just an attack of the human conscience. It is the Holy Spirit of God speaking to our hearts and leading us to receive Jesus Christ as our savior. We know what righteousness is, not just because the church has been proclaiming it for centuries, but because of the conviction of the Holy Spirit. Moreover, we are convicted that there will be a judgment because "the prince of this world now stands condemned," and he cannot win.

Jesus goes on to say that there is much yet for Him to teach His disciples, but that they are not ready for it yet; but when the Spirit comes into the world in Jesus' place, He will guide us into all truth when we are ready to receive it.

So then, the Christian life is first and foremost a life of actually following Jesus Christ who is alive and at work in our world and in the heart of each and every believer. Jesus Himself teaches us this truth in these passages of His final discourse in John's Gospel.

Much of the writings of the New Testament are directed at teaching and encouraging believers in their walk with Christ. Many had been faithful. Many more had become discouraged and had lost their edge. I am sure that for some, their faith had become dormant as the cares of this life had overwhelmed them. I found myself in this category when I first began my life on the road. Perhaps you find yourself in this place too. If you do, I encourage you to get back into His word, and into prayer, and into the fellowship of the believers. We will talk about these things more specifically in later chapters, but before we go on to talk about spiritual gifts, let me remind you of the words of the apostle Paul to the Colossians and to us:

> And now, just as you accepted Christ Jesus as your Lord, you must
> continue to follow him. Let your roots grow down into him, and
> let your lives be built on him. Then your faith will grow strong in

the truth you were taught, and you will overflow with thankfulness. Don't let anyone capture you with empty philosophies and high-sounding nonsense that come from human thinking and from the spiritual powers of this world, rather than from Christ. For in Christ lives all the fullness of God in a human body. So you also are complete through your union with Christ, who is the head over every ruler and authority. (Col. 2:6-10, NLT)

In this world today, there is a cacophony of voices that would capture our minds and our spirits with "empty philosophies and high-sounding nonsense that comes from human thinking and from the spiritual powers of this world, rather than from Christ." Let us get back in touch with the Spirit of Christ and follow Him rather than these.

Spiritual Gifts

We often talk of a person as being "gifted." For instance, one of my daughters, throughout her (quite lengthy) career as a student, was enrolled in several of what were referred to as classes for "gifted students." We also speak of "gifted" musicians and writers and many others usually in what we refer to as "the arts." Yet this is not what the Bible talks of when it speaks of "spiritual gifts." That which we also refer to as "talents," in which a person seems to have a particular ability in some area, are not "gifts" in a spiritual sense. These talents seem to be present in believers and unbelievers alike and are not necessarily given by God, except in the sense that He makes us all what we are and what we become.

The spiritual gifts that the Bible talks about, on the other hand, are *specific special abilities given to followers of Jesus Christ by the Holy Spirit, for the purpose of building up the Body of Christ.* The idea of "talents," as mentioned above, are often *vehicles* through which spiritual gifts can be expressed, yet they are not spiritual gifts themselves in the biblical sense. For instance, one can be a talented writer, but their writing talent is a means by which they may express the spiritual gifts of wisdom or special knowledge or prophecy or some other of the biblical spiritual gifts.

I need to say at the outset that I am *not* what is commonly called a "charismatic." I do, however, believe firmly in what the Bible teaches about the gifts of the Holy Spirit.

There are five passages of scripture that provide us of "lists" of spiritual gifts. None of these, even the two in 1 Corinthians 12, are identical. There are, however, several from each list that overlap. These five passages are

- 1 Corinthians 12:8-10,
- 1 Corinthians 12:28,
- Ephesians 4:11,
- Romans 12: 6-8, and
- 1 Peter 4:11. (This passage is not so much a "list" as it is the mentioning of two gifts as examples of the attitude with which all gifts should be exercised.)

It is not my purpose here to get into an extensive description of these spiritual gifts or the discussion of whether there are other gifts that are not mentioned. Nor is it my task to get us into the debate that has gone on for centuries regarding whether certain of these gifts have "ceased" and, if so, which ones. My intent here is simply to point out that following the Holy Spirit in our lives includes the discovery and the exercise of the gifts of the Spirit.[4]

Does every believer have a spiritual gift? There are at least the three scriptures which address this very issue:

> A spiritual gift is given to each of us so we can help each other.
> (1 Corinthians 12:7, NLT)

This verse precedes the list of spiritual gifts in 1 Corinthians 12: 8-10. The next verse is, of course, the one that follows that same list.

> All these are the work of one and the same Spirit, and he gives them
> to each one, just as he determines. (1 Corinthians 12:11, NIV)

This verse is then followed by a paragraph that talks about the body having many parts and how they must function together. So then, the greater context of these verses indicates that every believer has at least one, and perhaps several spiritual gifts, that they are to apply "so that the body of Christ may be built up" (Ephesians 4:12, NIV).

The following passage in 1 Peter also is found immediately preceding the verse cited above in the "lists." Peter tells us here,

God has given each of you a gift from his great variety of spiritual gifts. Use them well to serve one another. (4:10, NLT)

You will note the recurrence of the word "each" in all of these passages. It should be obvious at this point that I believe that indeed we are *each* given one or more spiritual gifts. The contexts of the scriptures are very clear that the purpose of these gifts are primarily for the building up, not of ourselves and our personal lives, but for the building up of the church, the Body of Christ.

A very important part of living our life in the Spirit is the discovering and developing of our spiritual gifts. We each need to make it a matter of prayer to try to find the opportunities we need both to learn of our spiritual gifts and to develop them in God's service. That, of course, brings us back to that which we have already discussed, the leadership of God's Holy Spirit in our lives.

I do feel it necessary to point out the danger of what we used to call "pigeonholing," that is, the practice of defining something in a narrow and restrictive way. Nowadays we use the term "thinking outside the box" as an antithesis to this idea. In the matter of spiritual gifts, let us beware of too rigidly defining what God wants us to do and how He wants us to apply those spiritual gifts that He has given us. It is less important to define our spiritual gifts than it is to do what God leads us to do and to allow Him to endow us with the necessary gifts to carry out the task at hand. Perhaps He has given us more than one gift to use in His service. Perhaps He has given us gifts that we are unaware of until we get into the situations for which they are needed. We will never be aware of what our gifts are until we learn to follow the leading of His Spirit in our daily lives.

For instance, we who are "seniors" often like to view ourselves as the wise sage due to our extensive life experience and the fact that younger folks frequently look up to us. It is easy for us to entertain a belief that the Spirit has given us the gift of uttering a "word of wisdom" (1 Corinthians 12:8). Those who would decide that this is their gift might simply look for opportunities to utter wisdom (though we may not possess as much of it as we would like to think). What we need to be doing, however, is to be about seeking the will of God regarding what tasks He would have us do in His Kingdom. If, in the context of these tasks, God uses us to speak a word of wisdom, then we have rightly exercised our spiritual gift.

The Fruit of the Spirit

What does a life that is led by the Spirit look like? Jesus said, "By their fruits you will know them" (Matthew 7:20, NKJV). Paul tells us in Galatians,

> But the Holy Spirit produces this kind of fruit in our lives: love, joy, peace, patience, kindness, goodness, faithfulness, gentleness, and self-control. There is no law against these things! (Galatians 5:22-23, NLT)

Of course, we need to remember that fruit is brought forth in maturity. Sometimes when it is young, a tree will bear no fruit at first, and then only a little fruit. With maturity and proper care, however, it will later bring forth an abundant harvest.

Contrast this, however, with what he says about the fruit that is borne in the life of the natural man:

> When you follow the desires of your sinful nature, the results are very clear: sexual immorality, impurity, lustful pleasures, idolatry, sorcery, hostility, quarreling, jealousy, outbursts of anger, selfish ambition, dissension, division, envy, drunkenness, wild parties, and other sins like these. (Galatians 5: 19-21, NLT)

So then, the Christian life is first and foremost a life of intimate fellowship with Jesus Christ. It is a life of following Him by the leading of His Spirit. It is a life in which we are members of His body and gifted by Him to use our gifts in the building up of His body, the church. It is a life in which He leads us away from the "natural man" who exercised the fruits of the sinful nature and toward the Christlike spiritual person whose life yields an abundant harvest of the fruit of the Holy Spirit.

CHAPTER 3

What Is "The Church"?
(A Brief Theology)

> Simon Peter answered, "You are the Christ, the Son of the living
> God."
>
> Jesus replied, "Blessed are you, Simon son of Jonah, for this
> was not revealed to you by man, but by my Father in heaven.
> And I tell you that you are Peter, and on this rock I will build my
> church, and the gates of Hades will not overcome it.
> —Matthew 16:16-18 (NIV)

IN THE FIRST chapter, I mentioned that early in my life on the road as a full-timer, I began to sense that the Lord was speaking to my heart about getting involved once again in the fellowship of believers. As I set out to actually do this, I began to wonder about several issues, such as:

Just what is "*The* Church"?

How important is it to be attached to a particular body of believers?

Is it wrong to be out here on the road, rather than being "planted" in the same congregation each week?

Does it matter if I "play hooky" from church occasionally? What about if I missed church regularly?

As I talk to other full-time RVers, I am finding that one of the things that concerns them most regarding the Christian life is their relationship to the body of believers. In this chapter, I would like us to take a look at some of the things that the Bible says about what the church is and what is every believer's relationship to it.

While I said in the first chapter that this is not simply a book about going to church while on the road, it is essential that a large part of the discussion center on the nature of "*The* Church." In fact, there can be no discussion of the Christian life without talking about our relationship to, and our concept of, the church.

So how do we define "The Church"? How do we come to an understanding of what it is?

First, let us look at the word that is translated into English as "church." As I'm sure many of us already know, the word translated as "church" in the New Testament is the Greek word *ekklesia*. It meant "to call out" or "those who are called out."[5] It described an assembly (think back to high school) or a meeting. It also described a congregation or synagogue when applied to the Jewish tradition. This is not particularly helpful to us, however, for ever since Jesus used the word as we see it recorded in Matthew 16:18, it would begin to take on a meaning far beyond anything it had ever had before.

Some Accepted but Not-So-Useful Definitions of "The Church"

Many of us have been taught to think of the church in terms of three contexts in which the word *ekklesia* is used in the New Testament (preachers throughout the centuries have been fond of dividing great truths into "threes"):

- *The Universal Church,* which consists of all believers, both those currently alive and those who are with the Lord. It also includes any who will come to believe in the future from now until the Lord returns.
- *The Visible Church,* which consists of all believers currently living on the earth at this moment.
- *The Local Church,* which consists of a local congregation in a particular group that meets in a particular geographic location and the members of that local congregation.

While I take no issue with this "triune" idea, I don't think that it is particularly helpful to us either in understanding what the church is or, more specifically, our own relationship to the church.

Also, to these three I think that modern times have added a fourth, generalized concept to our understanding. I call this *the institutional church.* This is a largely secular concept that social scientists and news commentators use when they refer to "*The* church" (although we will use the term "*The* Church" in a different way in the pages that follow). This is frequently a reference used by those who are outside the church, looking in, and it refers to what they see. It can alternately mean either all the people who attend church services with any degree of regularity and loosely subscribe to the moral teachings of some particular Christian church, or it can also be used to refer specifically to the Roman Catholic Church. In the secular humanist point of view, there is no real difference between the Roman Catholic Church and the various other church bodies of the Protestant tradition. Any concept of a spiritual church led by the very Spirit of the Living God is coincidental, if not foreign to this point of view.

I have talked to many Christians who are active church members who subconsciously accept this view of the church. I once viewed the church that way myself before I began to study the Bible more earnestly. This will not be our point of view if we are to come to a proper understanding of the church, but we do need to be aware of it and the way that it has become the popular definition within our secular culture.

So let us set all of these definitions aside for now and come up with a more useful way of viewing that body we call "*The* Church" and of looking at our relationship to it.

Beware of "Scholars"

It is not my intent to set forth at this point a "scholarly" discussion of the theology of the church. Yet this discussion must be, by its very nature, a theological discussion. But don't let this fact scare you away.

I am continually puzzled by the apparently popular belief that only "scholars" are able to arrive at reasonable conclusions about theological understanding and that, if one presents credentials as a "scholar," their word about whatever they are expounding should be accepted without question. And certainly, in our day, we have an adequate number of such scholars who are willing to offer their opinions.

When we use the term "scholar" or "theologian," we frequently conjure up the image of thick-spectacled, leather-elbowed, white-haired individuals with numerous degrees on the walls of their cluttered offices. When they speak, it is in a language barely discernable as English, using terms we have scarcely, if ever, uttered in our daily conversations.

I will have to say at the outset that I do not consider myself to be a "scholar," nor do I consider it necessary to be a scholar to engage in this discussion. Although I was once a theological student, and I have continued to study theology as a layman, I do not claim to be a theologian. I believe, however, that it is not necessary to be a so-called theologian to understand theology.

I believe in the idea that the Bible in the English language (or in whatever language you are reading) is the inerrant word of God. I am eternally grateful for all those who study the Bible and formulate the truths of the Bible into what we call "systematic theology." Theirs, if they truly belong to Jesus Christ, is an invaluable mission in the Kingdom of God. Let us not forget, however, that, as we said in the last chapter, it is the Holy Spirit who is our teacher and guide as we attempt to understand theological truth. Jesus said,

> But the Counselor, the Holy Spirit, whom the Father will send in my name, will teach you all things and will remind you of everything I have said to you. (John 14:26, NIV)

Let us remember the important truth that God *wants* to communicate with us! It is not through scholars but through His Holy Spirit, the eternal Word Himself, that God wants to speak to us through His word, the scriptures.

There is a marvelous story that takes place in the third and the beginning parts of the fourth chapter of the book of Acts. Peter and John are going to the temple in Jerusalem for the traditional afternoon prayer service. They are stopped by a crippled beggar who asks them for money. This is the famous passage where Peter says, "Silver and gold have I none, but that which I have I give you. In the name of Jesus Christ of Nazareth, rise up and walk" (Acts 3:6). The man is, of course, healed. The crowd is astonished, and Peter, seeing his opportunity, begins to proclaim that it was in fact this man's faith in Jesus Christ by which he was healed. Then, like any good preacher in such a situation, he begins to proclaim the risen Jesus Christ, the Messiah, to them.

Enter the priests and the Sadducees, along with the temple guards, who proceeded to put them in jail. In the morning, they were brought before the high council (scholars), who demanded, "By what power, or in whose name have you done this?" (Acts 4:7, NLT).

Then Peter, "filled with the Holy Spirit," began to proclaim Jesus to them. I love the way that the New International Version records the reaction of the "scholars" to this meeting with Peter and John:

> When they saw the courage of Peter and John and realized that they were unschooled, ordinary men, they were astonished and they took note that these men had been with Jesus. (Acts 4:13, NIV)

It was not the scholars but the ordinary men and women who "had been with Jesus" who turned the first-century world upside down. The scholars, if anything, served as anchors that held these first Christians back. Of all the writers of the New Testament, the apostle Paul seems to be the only real "Bible scholar" in the bunch. Out of the entire Christian church of the first century, there is little said to indicate that more than a handful of such "scholars" as Paul were involved in the expansion of the church.

In our own day, scholarship has a different focus than it did back then; but in this day, as it was then, scholars frequently can be more a hindrance than a help in living the Christian life.

I believe that diligent study of God's word at the guidance of the Holy Spirit is the beginning and end of all theological understanding. It is in this setting that I offer my remarks that follow.

Having said that, I will offer a couple of quotes from actual theologians during the course of the discussion that follows in order to illustrate what we are saying and so that you will know that my ideas are not just those of some eccentric guy sitting in front of his laptop in a motor home.

A Brief Theology of the Church

What we are actually going to do here, when we say we are going to consider a "brief theology of the church," is, in fact, to take a look at what the Bible says about this subject. This is not an exhaustive look at *everything* that the Bible says on the subject of the church but a look at some of the scriptures that will help us to understand the nature of the church in the context of what it means to us as full-time RVers to be members of the Body of Christ.

So come, become a "theologian" with me for a few moments as we look to the scriptures regarding the church.

Many have sought to define the church throughout the years and have found their attempts to be inadequate. We who *are* the church can readily see the inadequacy of these attempts to define just what this Body of which we are members really is. There are many passages in the New Testament that describe some aspect of the nature and function of the church. Perhaps it is because of this broad range of references that we find it difficult to be concise about defining the church.

Perhaps it is best to begin by going back to that first recorded teaching of Jesus about the church that we used as our text for this chapter. Since it is so many pages back, I will repeat it here once again, along with its immediate context, for the reader's convenience.

> When Jesus came to the region of Caesarea Philippi, he asked his disciples, "Who do people say the Son of Man is?"
>
> They replied, "Some say John the Baptist; others say Elijah; and still others, Jeremiah or one of the prophets."
>
> "But what about you?" he asked. "Who do you say I am?"
>
> Simon Peter answered, "You are the Christ, the Son of the living God."
>
> Jesus replied, "Blessed are you, Simon son of Jonah, for this was not revealed to you by man, but by my Father in heaven. And I tell you that you are Peter, and on this rock I will build my church, and the gates of Hades will not overcome it. (Matthew 16:13-18, NIV)

Who Owns "*The* Church"?

The first thing I want us to notice about this passage is that Jesus declares to us that this is *His* church! It is *not* an organization which the disciples founded after His ascension to keep themselves together or to provide them the structure they needed to reach out to the world. It is the church of Jesus Christ, and no matter what they may think, no particular denomination (or "nondenomination") holds a copyright to that title. It is His church, and His alone.

> In his book *Basic Christian Doctrine*, Dr. John H. Leith makes the following comments:
>
> Nowhere in the New Testament is there the slightest indication that the Church . . . came into being by human plans. Everywhere . . . the actions of the Christian Community indicate that the believers suddenly found themselves to be a community without ever planning to be.[6]

If you think about it as you examine the record in the book of Acts and the other postresurrection writings of the New Testament, you begin to realize that this truth is obvious.

The church had its beginning in the group of people who followed Jesus during His earthly ministry. We often think only of "the twelve" as His disciples, but if we pay attention to the New Testament, we realize that there were a sizable number of people who followed him both regularly and intermittently. The word *ekklesia* is not used until later, in the book of Acts; but this group, many of whom perhaps were originally followers of John the Baptist, were among the group from which came the believers upon whom the Holy Spirit fell at Pentecost.

One could say that the actual act of "building" the church probably began when Jesus uttered these words above and called them His "church" for the first time. There were no recorded "organizational meetings" before Pentecost. Only about 120 men and women huddled together in prayer, not really knowing what was going to happen. They knew that Jesus had told them to wait in Jerusalem and that there they would be baptized with the Holy Spirit. They probably didn't know what this meant or how it would take place.

The story in Acts of the great movement of the Holy Spirit on the day of Pentecost is presented to us as an event that was entirely a work of God. Men were not the prime movers of this great event but simply the yielded vessels through which He chose to work that day. The picture of the church that Luke presents in Acts is one of a continuation of the disciples following Jesus, and submitting to His Lordship and leading. The entire event of Pentecost, as well as everything else that happens in the book of Acts, is presented as a work of God Himself rather than the "Acts" and decisions of the men and women that made up the church.

> Dr. Leith goes on further to say,

> In this way too, the church differs from human organizations, which in a real sense belong to the organizers who set the rules. In the church Jesus Christ is Lord, and to Him the community owes its unqualified allegiance.[7]

> He also reminds us,

The church is a community that acknowledges Jesus Christ as Lord. The first creed of the church was "Jesus is Lord."[8]

Or as Paul states so clearly in Romans,

If you confess with your mouth, "Jesus is Lord," and believe in your heart that God raised him from the dead, you will be saved. (Romans 10:9, NIV)

Yet another reason that we are compelled to see the church as a work of God, and not of men, is the fact that it thrived in an environment in which all odds were against its survival. In the fourteenth chapter of the book of Acts, when Paul and Barnabas's first missionary journey drew to an end, we read,

Paul and Barnabas also appointed elders in every church. With prayer and fasting, they turned the elders over to the care of the Lord, in whom they had put their trust. (Acts 14: 23, NLT)

Paul and Barnabas had been with the believers in these churches for such a short time! They appointed the "elders" (the word seems singularly inappropriate as they were so new to the Christian faith), and with very little training, they "turned them over to the care of the Lord." Yet as time goes on, we find that these churches continued to grow. This is yet further evidence that the early church was a work of the Holy Spirit and not a work of man. The growth of the church in the first years of its life defies all theories that we hold about organizational growth. There is simply no reason why it should not have died off except for the work of the Holy Spirit!

All Christians Are Members of the Church

In the passage above, Jesus declares to Peter, "You are Peter [which means 'rock'] and on this rock I will build my church." Some, mostly within the Roman Catholic tradition, have held this to mean that the church would be founded on the leadership of Peter himself. There is little support, however, for this position in the New Testament. The scriptures give no indication that Peter, dynamic leader though he was, was held in any greater esteem than the other apostles. Nor did he take a more prominent place of leadership than the others, except in the beginning chapters of Acts. It is inaccurate to say that Peter was any more influential than Paul, whose writings make up a very large part of the New Testament. In fact, Paul at one point took it upon himself to correct Peter when he felt that Peter was being hypocritical (Galatians 2:11-13).

In the Evangelical tradition, it is generally held that Jesus was referring to Peter's confession "You are the Messiah, the Son of the living God" (Matthew 16:16, NLT), as the rock upon which the church would be built.

I want to take that idea a step further and point out the words of Jesus that immediately follow Peter's confession. He says, "Blessed are you, Simon son of Jonah, for this was not revealed to you by man, but by my Father in heaven." Then Jesus says, "On this rock I will build my church" (17-18). So then, I interpret this to mean that the church is built on everyone to whom the living God has revealed that Jesus is His Son and Messiah. We can accurately say then that the church is made up of those who have found salvation in Jesus Christ. There are no other requirements, and there is no believer who is exempt. If you believe that Jesus Christ is your savior, you are a member of the church. Membership is automatic, and it is not optional.

The Church Is *One* Body of Believers

When we affirm that the church is one body, this is not just to say that the church *should* be one body, or that it should *strive* to be united as one, but that it is, in fact, one Body of Christ, and it cannot be anything else, myriads of denominations notwithstanding. We will talk more about denominations and differences and the significance of these in a moment, but let us hold fast to this one important fact: that all who know Jesus Christ as their Savior are one body.

The very metaphor of a body with its various parts working together in harmony gives us a picture of the church as one entity. The New Testament is emphatic about this point. Paul writes,

> As a prisoner for the Lord, then, I urge you to live a life worthy of the calling you have received. Be completely humble and gentle; be patient, bearing with one another in love. Make every effort to keep the unity of the Spirit through the bond of peace. There is one body and one Spirit—just as you were called to one hope when you were called—one Lord, one faith, one baptism; one God and Father of all, who is over all and through all and in all. (Ephesians 4:1-6, NIV)

Just as our bodies have many parts and each part has a special function, So it is with Christ's body. We are many parts of one body, and we all belong to each other. (Romans 12:4-5, NLT)

The human body has many parts, but the many parts make up one whole body. So it is with the body of Christ. Some of us are Jews, some are Gentiles, some are slaves, and some are free. But we have all been baptized into one body by one Spirit, and we all share the same Spirit. (1 Corinthians 12:12-13, NLT)

There are many other scriptures that echo this same concept of unity in Christ, but we need not go on. These are certainly enough for us to see that it is a major teaching in the New Testament that the church is one body.

Denominations do not so much represent disunity as they do diversity. I see them as a sort of "truth in labeling." If you enter a Baptist church or a Lutheran church or a Methodist church or a Pentecostal church, you know that you are going to have a similar experience to that which you would have in any other churches with those same labels in any other part of the world.

I do not see either that differences in opinion regarding minor doctrines are a threat to unity, except regarding the attitudes we may hold about those with whose opinions we differ. If the Jerusalem Council (Acts 15) is any indication, there have always been differences of opinion regarding doctrine within the church. The Good News of Christ is not about following a certain teaching but about the atoning death, the life-giving resurrection, and the empowering ascension of Jesus Christ.

I do not pretend that the differences that separate the various denominations are insignificant. I do not suggest that they would be easy to lay aside or even that they should be laid aside. I believe, however, that in spite of all these differences that separate the denominations, the Body of Christ is one body, led by one Spirit, and this is the church of Jesus Christ.

If we believe that we are saved by Christ's sacrifice on the cross and by the power of His resurrection, if we believe that Jesus is the Messiah, the Son of the Living God, we are individually members of His church, and together we are "*The* Church."

In her book *Here I Am Lord, Send Somebody Else*, Jill Briscoe tells the following story that illustrates what we see in the scriptures:

A man told me . . . "I've left the Church!" "You can't" I replied, "Church is not somewhere you go; Church is something you are, so you can't leave what you are. You are a member of the body of Christ! You can't amputate yourself from His Body."[9]

So then, let us understand "*The* Church" as the entire Body of Christ, similar in definition to the "universal church" that we mentioned at the beginning of the chapter.

It is frequently pointed out that in the New Testament, there are many more references to the "local church" than there are to the universal church, to which I would reply that quantity does not equal quality. The unfortunate fixation on the local church in many evangelical circles has often caused us to lose sight of the clear teaching of the Bible that the church is *the* Body of Christ, rather than an institution. Yet it poses an interesting question: If we truly understand "*The* Church" as the whole Body of Christ, or universal church, what then is to be our understanding of, and our relationship to, the local church?

"*The* Church" and "*a* Church"

While we have set forth a concept of "*The* Church" of which all believers are members, there are, both in the New Testament and in the life of the church, from the first to the twenty-first century, localized assemblies, which are expressions of the body of believers. Let us say then that there is "*The* Church," referring to the universal church, to which all believers belong, and then there is "*a* church," referring to the local church. It is the local church that we will discuss in the following chapter.

While it may be helpful to make these two divisions to aid our understanding, it is clear that these concepts alone are not inclusive enough to really put a finger on just what is the church. Perhaps it is precisely because we have sought to define the church that we have come to experience so much frustration in finding a clear and concise definition of it. Long ago, God declared to us through His prophet,

"For my thoughts are not your thoughts, neither are your ways my ways," declares the LORD. "As the heavens are higher than the earth, so are my ways higher than your ways and my thoughts than your thoughts." (Isaiah 55:8, NIV)

As in all cases of trying to describe God or His inventions, we are frustrated in our attempts both to fully conceptualize and to articulate a concept or a truth that originates with Almighty God Himself. If we are going to understand just what the church is, let us remember that we must first and foremost understand that the church, the *true* church, is an invention not of man but of God.

Second, it is important that we realize that the church is more than an aggregate of its members. It is the entire collection of believers and God, who has empowered them with His Holy Spirit and chosen them to carry out His work in the world.

Once we understand that we who are saved by the grace of God through the life, death, and resurrection of our Lord Jesus Christ are all members of *His* church, it is easier to understand what should be our relationship to "*a* church" or the local church.

CHAPTER 4

What Is "*a* Church"?

I am writing to God's church in Corinth, to you who have been called by God to be his own holy people. He made you holy by means of Christ Jesus, just as he did for all people everywhere who call on the name of our Lord Jesus Christ, their Lord and ours.
—1 Corinthians 1:2 (NLT)

O NE OF THE most difficult things for Christians who are living the full-time RV lifestyle to deal with is our relationship to the local church. We will deal with this matter in more detail later, but for now, we will make note of the fact that the question our relationship to the body of believers and its numerous local expressions is for most of us "the big question" when it comes to how we will go about living the Christian life on the road.

For many of us, and for most of our lives, going to church has been almost synonymous with living the Christian life. Our identity as a Christian revolved around which local church we attended, how often we attended, and what activities we were involved in at our local church. Most of us were identified with one particular denomination. For many of us, there was a ministry that we performed in our home congregations, such as being a deacon, a reader, an usher, a Sunday school teacher, and so on.

The above passage from 1 Corinthians comes as close as any to being a "definition in a verse" of what the local church is. Paul addresses himself to one particular local body who "have been called by God to be his own holy people" along with all others "everywhere" who have called on the name of our Lord Jesus Christ, "their Lord and ours." The local church, then, is a gathering of believers "who call on the name of our Lord Jesus Christ" and is a local presentation of the universal church. This is, of course, an oversimplification, but it is a good place to start.

As we ask ourselves the questions regarding what constitutes a proper local church, many of us are examining some of the "church" services conducted at our RV parks in light of the scriptures and of what we have been taught in the past and are wondering if they qualify as "real church." While I have an opinion about this, which I will get to later, I certainly do not have an answer with which everyone will universally agree.

If then the local church is a gathering of believers and a local presentation of the universal church as we have said, the question is raised, "is every local congregation that calls itself a 'church' really a church?" In most cases, the answer will be yes but unfortunately not in all.

Most of you who are reading this book will be like myself in that you have attended churches that historically grew out of the Protestant Reformation. We have come to think of what the true church is in terms of what the Reformers thought about it. The Reformers, particularly Luther and Calvin, insisted that the characteristics that constituted a true church were

a. that the word of God was rightly preached, and
b. that the sacraments were rightly administered.[10]

And while these were helpful to them in their day, especially as they sought to justify their actions, and to differentiate between themselves and the Roman Catholic Church from which they broke away, they are somewhat inadequate for us as we seek to define what a local church is and should be.

The second characteristic above, that of the "sacraments," is particularly difficult to apply. Certainly, the local church is, and rightly should be, a setting in which these "sacraments" are administered, but is the manner in which the "sacraments" are administered really a proper evidence of a true church?

First of all, there is no general agreement among Evangelical Christians about the number and meaning of the "sacraments," although all generally agree that baptism and the Lord's Supper are included. Also, many Evangelical churches insist on calling them "ordinances" rather than "sacraments," the latter word suggesting that they may be acts performed to obtain merit with God.

Also, there is much difference of opinion as to how the "sacraments" should be administered and what their meaning is. Should baptism be administered by immersion, sprinkling, or pouring? Should it be administered to infants, children, adults, or "all of the above?" Regarding the Lord's Supper, how often should it be administered, and to whom? Should each individual partake of the elements as they are served to him, or should we follow Paul's admonition and "wait for each other" (1 Corinthians 11:33) and partake all together at the same moment?

Since we cannot agree on what constitutes the "rightly administered sacraments," how much "wrongly" administration of the sacraments can we tolerate if we are to judge the trueness or falseness of a local church by this standard? Do any of us dare to judge a local group of believers on the basis of whether they observe the sacraments or ordinances according to our own view of what these mean and how they should be conducted? And what of such groups as the Salvation Army who practice neither baptism nor the Lord's Supper? Dare we say that those believers who gather in their "citadels" to worship our Lord Jesus Christ each Sunday do not constitute a church?

The same problem enters in when we attempt to judge whether, and to what degree, the "word is rightly preached."

Obviously, there is a line of demarcation at this point, which cannot be crossed and the congregation still be considered a church. Paul said to the Galatians,

> If we, or an angel from heaven, preach any other gospel to you than what we have preached to you, let him be accursed. (Galatians 1:8, NKJV)

Yet how wrong is too wrong to still be considered a true church? We have many denominations in Christendom today simply because we cannot agree on interpretation of scripture. Is true interpretation of scripture, or doctrinal purity, a true yardstick by which to measure what is a true church?

What if the man in the pulpit does not believe in or preach the true Gospel of Jesus Christ but the congregation still believes and teaches it, or vice versa? What if the denomination or leading representatives of it have forsaken the Gospel but individuals in a particular congregation still believe and teach it?

As much as we may esteem the Reformers and the work they did to bring the church into the focus of its true center, we cannot really apply a doctrinal test to determine what makes a local church a true church. This brings us back to our starting point, that of the local church being a representation of the universal church.

The Characteristics of a Church

Perhaps the most useful thing we can do to understand what a "true" local church is, is to describe what happens in a true local church. What are the "characteristics of a local church"? What are the "functions of a local church"?

A Church Contains Believers

A true church must contain members of the universal church. If the universal church is the body of all those who have been saved by the grace of our Lord Jesus Christ, then the local church must also be made up of these same believers in order to be considered a true church. This is not to say that everyone who is a member of a local church will be a true believer. Jesus said that the wheat must grow together with the tares (Matthew 13:24-30) and that He would separate the sheep from the goats when He comes to judge the nations (Matthew 25:31-46). Yet we cannot consider a church to be a true church unless it offers full membership only to those redeemed in Christ.

A Church Will Be about Jesus Christ

Remember that we said in the last chapter that the church belongs to our Lord Jesus Christ and that it is His body. A true church must espouse the idea, at least, that Christ is its head and that they are about Jesus Christ, "the Son of the living God." A congregation teaching that Jesus Christ is not alive and is not the Savior of each and all and that He did not rise from the dead simply cannot be considered a true church. Such "churches" as the Unitarian Church cannot be considered a true church simply because their teaching has no connection with the saving and risen Jesus Christ.

A Church Should Be Led by the Holy Spirit

A true church *should* also display some evidence that the Holy Spirit is at work, at some level, in their midst. I say "should" because it is possible for a congregation to shut out the Holy Spirit. When congregations shut out the Spirit of God, the egos of men take over, and the church becomes a forum for those who are in love with the sound of their own voice.

Dr. W. L. Muncy[11] was fond of telling the story about a young man with a "learning disability" who presented himself for membership in a certain local church. The pastor, being uncertain about whether this young man should be a church member, told him to "go home and pray about it" with the hope that he would forget about it in time. After several days, the young man presented himself again for membership in the church. The pastor asked him, "Did you pray about it?" to which the young man replied in the affirmative. The pastor then asked him, "And what did the Lord tell you?"

To which the young man replied, "He said to just keep trying, because He's been trying to get into this church Himself for years!"

My friends Lynn Johnson and Becky Linn of Follow Hard Ministries quote in one of their brochures a saying by A. W. Tozer that if God were to take the Holy Spirit out of this world, most of what the church is doing would go right on and nobody would know the difference!

We like to joke about these things, but a church without the leadership of the Holy Spirit is no joke! We said in our study of His farewell discourse in chapter 2, it is the intention of our Lord Jesus that we be led by His Spirit. Nowhere is this more urgently necessary than in the local church.

A Church Has an Intent to Function as a Church

During my career in law enforcement, an important factor that was always of prime consideration in determining whether a criminal act had been committed was that of *intent.* The difference between something as important as murder, manslaughter, or accidental death was that of the intent of the person who committed the act.

So what is the difference between a "house church" and a home Bible study? What is the difference between a meeting of a local church and a meeting of Youth for Christ or some similar parachurch group? It is *the intent to function as a church.*

Perhaps, then, it is important to see what the functions of a church look like and what it means to "function as a church."

The Functions of a Church

I have spent most of my Christian life in church environments that sought to emulate the New Testament model of faith and practice as closely as possible. Having said that, I must say that I do not feel that it is really necessary that we seek to be carbon copies of the church that we see in the New Testament as far as our practices and forms are concerned. It has always been surprising to me that the New Testament is amazingly silent about many of the specifics regarding how they carried out their meetings, or how each body was individually governed. There always seems to be a leader, some form of what we would regard as a pastor and a group of "elders" that were present. Otherwise, there is little to indicate that things were exactly the same in each local church. I think that it is safe to assume that those local congregations that were led by Jewish believers followed the Jewish patterns they were accustomed to in their synagogues, at least in the beginning, but perhaps the leaders and the people just kind of went with whatever worked best for them.[12]

What is more important is what goes on inside the meetings of a local church. The following items are not intended to be an exhaustive list of the functions of a church. Indeed, they are not even intended to be a list of functions that must only occur in a local church. As I hope we saw in the last chapter, the Body of Christ is a very comprehensive organism. What I intend to put forth here is several features that will be a part of what goes on in a local fellowship of believers.

Worship

There can be little question that a major function of the local church is that of corporate worship. Paul admonished the church at Colossae:

> Let the peace of Christ rule in your hearts, since as members of one body you were called to peace. And be thankful. Let the word of Christ dwell in you richly as you teach and admonish one another with all wisdom, and as you sing psalms, hymns and spiritual songs with gratitude in your hearts to God. (Colossians 3:15-16, NIV)

Expressions of praise and gratitude, prayer, admonishing and teaching from the word, singing "psalms, hymns, and spiritual songs"—these are among the elements of our worship experience as we meet together with our brothers and sisters in Christ.

Administration of Baptism and the Lord's Supper

It is also safe to say that instances of baptism (with the exception of Philip and the Ethiopian in Acts 8) and of the Lord's Supper were generally performed in the New Testament under the auspices of the local churches. In fact, on those occasions that Paul takes it upon himself to instruct the churches on the proper observance of the Lord's Supper, he emphasizes that it is something that the local church is to observe as a group. The most notable of these is his teaching in 1 Corinthians 11, verses 17 and following.

While I do not suggest that observances of the Lord's Supper outside the local church are necessarily wrong or inappropriate, I do suggest that these observances are an essential part of the local church's function and that the local congregation is the normal context in which these will occur.

Building Up the Body of Christ

One of the primary functions of the local church is promoting Christian growth. This is one reason why it is so important that we all be a part of a local congregation and why it is so important that the local churches be diligent to perform this task. When we discussed spiritual gifts, we looked at this passage in Ephesians that gave us one of our partial lists of spiritual gifts; we found that it also told us the purpose of those gifts.

> Now these are the gifts Christ gave to the church: the apostles, the prophets, the evangelists, and the pastors and teachers. Their responsibility is to equip God's people to do his work and build up the church, the body of Christ. This will continue until we all come to such unity in our faith and knowledge of God's Son that we will be mature in the Lord, measuring up to the full and complete standard of Christ.
>
> Then we will no longer be immature like children. We won't be tossed and blown about by every wind of new teaching. We will not be influenced when people try to trick us with lies so clever they sound like the truth. Instead, we will speak the truth in love, growing in every way more and more like Christ, who is the head of his body, the church. He makes the whole body fit together perfectly. As each part does its own special work, it helps the other parts grow, so that the whole body is healthy and growing and full of love. (Ephesians 4:11-16, NLT)

This passage then tells us that the purposes of these spiritual gifts are to equip the believers for their ministry to the world and to bring about Christian maturity, "growing in every way more and more like Christ." I like to call this particular list of spiritual gifts in Ephesians 4 the "pastoral gifts" as they are functions that in our own day we associate with "professional clergy." The local church then will be the context in which we will most frequently see persons exercising these gifts.

I acknowledge without reservation that Christian growth occurs in many contexts other than in a local church, yet this should be a primary function within every local body.

Exercising of the Spiritual Gifts

If the purpose of these spiritual gifts is to build up the Body of Christ, then the local expressions of the Body of Christ, the local churches, are the place in which these will be predominantly put to use. This is not to say that they will not have a use outside of the local church. The Body of Christ, as we repeatedly have suggested, is not confined within the walls of a building; but when members of a local body of believers exercise their spiritual gifts outside of the confines of a congregational meeting, they are functioning as members of the whole church in general and also of their own local body in particular.

Ordination and Authorization

While, to New Testament, practice of "laying on of hands" was far more widely applied than for just setting apart certain persons for a particular type of service, it seems clear that they did practice a form of what we today would call "ordination" in some cases.[13] Today we have traditionally practiced ordination of deacons and of professional clergy. This type of "laying on of hands" was a local church function in the New Testament as it is in many denominational traditions today. To recognize those who are gifted in these tasks and functions is a part of what is appropriate to the local church.

A great many forms of ministry take place both inside and outside the local church. It is important that the local churches authorize or validate these in some way, particularly when their own members are involved. This is how we know that these are not a part of the "wind of new teaching . . . and . . . lies so clever they sound like the truth" that Paul talks about in the passage above.

Again, for the part of us that is the natural man, we resist being subject to scrutiny for someone else's approval, but it is an important thing to be recognized and approved by our fellow believers who are in the Spirit. This is an appropriate function of the whole church in general and the local church in particular.

Fellowship

Do you ever feel like you're all alone out there? I certainly do sometimes. When I found my way back into the fellowship of believers, one of the most overwhelming feelings came with the realization that I was not alone out there, and that there were many like-minded brothers and sisters who were following the Holy Spirit in their daily lives.

Paul gives us a picture of what the fellowship of a local church looks like in these words to the local church at Colossae:

> Therefore, as God's chosen people, holy and dearly loved, clothe yourselves with compassion, kindness, humility, gentleness, and patience. Bear with each other and forgive whatever grievances you may have against one another. Forgive as the Lord forgave you. And over all these virtues put on love, which binds them all together in perfect unity.
>
> Let the peace of Christ rule in your hearts, since as members of one body you were called to peace. And be thankful. Let the word of Christ dwell in you richly as you teach and admonish one another with all wisdom, and as you sing psalms, hymns and spiritual songs with gratitude in your hearts to God. (Colossians 3: 12-16, NIV)
>
> And in Galatians 6:2 he further tells us,
>
> Carry each other's burdens, and in this way you will fulfill the law of Christ. (NIV)

Ministry to the World

The word "outreach" has almost become a cliché when used by churches. Our ministry to a world in need is an undeniable responsibility. It is through our local congregations that generally we find opportunity to involve ourselves in this type of ministry.

The Celebration Methodist Church of Brandon, South Dakota, adopted a slogan for the year 2007: "The church has left the building." And they devised several ways to take their ministry out into the community. All local churches should seek ways to impact their community beyond the walls of their buildings.

Winning the Lost

This could be regarded as a part of the "ministry to the world" above, except that it is so unique and so important that it needs to be mentioned separately. Those who are redeemed by Christ are the only ones who can carry the message of redemption into the world. I know many churches that are so poor financially that they can barely afford to pay their own bills, let alone pay the cost of many of the outreach programs that the more affluent churches are able to do. But these churches can still faithfully proclaim the Gospel of salvation. Jesus said,

> What do you benefit if you gain the whole world but lose your own soul? (Mark 8:36, NLT)

Indeed, what is the benefit if we, as the people of God, in our ministry to the world, feed the hungry, shelter the homeless, clothe the naked, finance the poor, give medical assistance to the sick, and in general make the lives of the "less fortunate" better but fail to proclaim to the world in the process the one message that will heal the sickness that is in everyone? What does it profit them indeed if they gain all these physical things but lose their souls?

That this soul-winning ministry be carried on by the local church is essential because each person, as we have repeatedly observed, has a different function to perform in this. Not all can be the evangelist who directly leads one to salvation in Christ, but as the Body of Christ functions as a whole, everyone has a part in this function.

As I told in the first chapter, I was not "led to the Lord" by any one person's witness, but as I look back now, I can see that my response to the prompting of the Holy Spirit was a result of both spoken and unspoken testimony from many people.

Preserving the Faith

Jude urges us to "contend for the faith that was once for all entrusted to the saints" (Jude 1:3, NIV). A very real function of the local church is that of preserving the faith. While all of us may not necessarily agree on the details, we should all have a commitment to preserving the truth and integrity of God's revelation of Himself in the Bible and in His Son, Jesus Christ. We are particularly responsible for upholding the essential truth of the saving death and bodily resurrection of our Lord Jesus.

Accountability

No one especially wants to be accountable to someone else, although we are usually all right with the idea of them being accountable to us. This is a part of the natural man. Yet a key part of what happens in a church is that we are accountable to Jesus Christ, and as a result, we are to hold one another accountable to Him and the standards imposed by His word. Paul said,

> Brothers, if someone is caught in a sin, you who are spiritual should restore him gently. But watch yourself, or you also may be tempted. Carry each other's burdens, and in this way you will fulfill the law of Christ. (Galatians 6:1-2, NIV)

The burden here is on those who are "spiritual." There has been a degree of abuse of this concept throughout the history of the church and especially in contemporary times. The egos of men have a way of finding their way into the fellowship of God's people, and the "unspiritual" are all too eager to exercise power and to create the power struggles that result. This is a touchy thing, but it is a necessary part of what Jesus intended His church to do. We must hold one another accountable, and accountability must work both ways, both from the leadership and toward the leadership of a congregation.

While the enemy has used this part of our natural man and exploited it to produce disunity among us, the holding of each other accountable to Christ is a necessary part of what we are to do as a local church.

The Body of Christ

When we separate the functions of a local church for analysis, as we have just done, we are at risk of thinking of the church as an *organization* rather than an *organism*. It is, as we have previously said, the Body of Christ. This is where all the parts of the body come together and perform their individual functions in harmony, with Christ as the directing head of the body and in the power of the life-giving Holy Spirit. This is more than just a metaphor. This is what is really happening.

We are tempted to think of our local church as our Christian "support group" and this it is in a very functional way, yet as Dr. Leith reminds us,

> The church cannot be described simply as an aid or support. In a very basic way, life in the church is the life of the individual Christian. God, who calls us to be Christian, also calls us to be His people, that is, the church.[14]

We are, above all, the Body of Christ, and our function is to follow Him and to represent Him in the world.

Think Global; Act Local

We have seen then that the church, whether we are talking about the universal church or the local manifestations of it, is Christ's church and an invention of God Himself. Every believer is a member of Christ's church, and while not every local church will necessarily recognize each believer, indeed the local church is where form meets function for every believer. We all need a relationship with a local church if we are going to take our rightful place as a member of the Body of Christ.

In many of the sources that I researched for this chapter, there was a great deal that was said against a contemporary trend in "church hopping" and of the necessity for believers to commit themselves to one local congregation. In other words, there is a tendency for some folks to "shop around" for a church that "meets their needs."

Please understand. I believe that everyone ought to belong to one local congregation, somewhere, and we will talk about that in the next chapter; but if you think about it, we who are believers in Jesus Christ and who travel in our RVs are the ultimate church hoppers.

As we have pointed out in this chapter and the last, it is easier to conceptualize the local church than to conceptualize the "universal church." We say that we believe that the church is the Body of Christ. When we say that we are all members of one body, we mean that all believers are the "church."

Many times, we who travel in our RVs, and especially those of us who are full-timers, feel guilty that we do not remain in one local church every Sunday. Yet it is important that we realize that we are a part a larger body than any individual local congregation. We have a right to be in "our Father's house" anywhere we go. An important part of the Christian life is worshiping beside our brothers and sisters in Christ. Another important part is spending time hearing God's word preached and taught in fellowship with other Christians.

Regardless of where we are on Sunday morning, we should be a part of the fellowship of believers whenever possible. No matter what the sign says outside regarding denomination, if believers are inside and if God's word is being faithfully taught inside, it is our church (or perhaps we should say, it is His church).

Being an RV traveler opens up many opportunities for new and rewarding experiences within the community of believers.

At the same time, the greatest danger to the Christian full-timer is the danger of becoming a detached believer. I feel that it is of the utmost importance, especially when we are going to be somewhere for a longer period of time, to find a place—one specific place—to be a part of a specific fellowship of believers.

How then do we go about finding that one specific local body of believers? What are the criteria that we should use to select a local church to attend?

CHAPTER 5

Selecting a Local Church

Let us not give up meeting together, as some are in the habit of doing, but let us encourage one another—and all the more as you see the Day approaching.

—Hebrews 10:25 (NIV)

In our society even churches can become like marketplaces, and congregations can be characterized chiefly as consumers. The drive to satisfy every taste and opinion can distract the church from its center: Jesus Christ among us.[15]

I AM GOING to begin this chapter with a confession: I sometimes fail to make it to church. This is especially true in cases when we are in a community for a brief stopover on a single Sunday.

Please understand; I am not making excuses, nor am I trying to say this is the right thing to do. I am simply telling it like it is. For me, the most difficult part of trying to live the Christian life on the road is trying to motivate myself to walk into a group of strangers in an unfamiliar community, even if it is my Lord's house of worship. I am an introvert by nature, and I must continually fight my natural man to overcome this reluctance. And when I do, I am usually blessed for my effort.

The Emotional Factor

For me and, I am convinced, for many others, overcoming this emotional factor is a primary consideration in whether or not I make it to church on a given Sunday. I always imagine what might happen if the congregation of strangers doesn't receive me well or looks down on "outsiders." By now, I have gone to so many different congregations and have failed to have this happen that I should know that it is a trick that Satan is playing on my mind. There may be congregations out there where this might happen, but I have received a warm welcome wherever I have gone. I am convinced that a friendly reception is the norm in most churches rather than an imagined cold one, which is more the product of popular fiction than of reality.

I have also realized that the more consecutive Sundays I skip, the harder it is to get back going again. Regular church attendance is an act of worship, but it is also a habit—a good habit. And like all good habits, it is more difficult to establish and requires more cultivation than a bad habit. Its counterpart, the bad habit of nonattendance, simply requires that you do nothing, except perhaps to soothe your conscience by telling yourself, "Maybe next Sunday."

So why is it so important to be a part of a local fellowship of believers?

One recent summer, I heard a couple of my friends perform a song called "Just Jesus and Me." I hadn't heard this song in many years, and it reminded me of those earlier times in my Christian life. I reflected on what its message had meant to me when I first heard it in college days and what it means to me now. This song, I believe, was meant to put forth the personal nature of being a Christian. As we talked about in the first two chapters, personally encountering Jesus Christ and establishing a one-on-one relationship with Him and being personally guided in our life and personal mission by His Spirit is at the very heart of the Christian experience.

Back in the "hippie era" of the late '60s, when I was in college (no, I didn't have long hair, even back then), there came a trend toward "self-actualization," and we all started looking inward. It was one of those things that had a good side and a bad side. The good side was that we had fertile ground for telling people that they needed a "personal relationship" with God through Jesus Christ.

On the minus side of the ledger, we produced a generation that "did their own thing" and had a tendency to avoid any meaningful participation in anything that had to do with a group. "The Church," which we had come to define as the *institutional church* that we discussed back in chapter 3, was considered irrelevant by many and was given somewhat of a marginal status in the thinking of the day.

There is no substitute for personal faith in the Lord Jesus Christ and personally following the Holy Spirit in our lives. Yet there is another dimension to Jesus' plan for all of us His people.

In the book *Being the Body*, Charles Colson and Ellen Vaughn discuss the corporate nature of the Christian life. If you want a more thorough discussion of what it means to be a member of the Body of Christ, I suggest you read that book. At one point, they discuss Jesus' farewell discourse in the Gospel of John, and indeed how millions of believers have gone forth since that time and have been the church, the Body of Christ, in the world. I couldn't agree with them more when they make the statement

> If we don't grasp *the intrinsically corporate nature of Christianity* embodied in the Church, we are missing the very heart of Jesus' plan.[16]

The lone-wolf Christian is a figment of the imagination of the natural man. Jesus intended from the very beginning that His church would be a fellowship, a family, carrying out His mission as a group effort by the power of His Spirit.

There is simply a dimension of the Christian experience of which we cannot partake alone. Add to this all the "functions of a local church" that we talked about in the last chapter, which we would miss if we were not a part of a local congregation. And above all this, can any one of us honestly say that it is God's will for their life that they *not* be a part of a local church?

We have seen that we are all members of His church. We have determined that we have a right, a reason, and indeed a responsibility to be in our Father's house, and to serve alongside our brothers and sisters in a local congregation. So what does this mean to us as we travel, and how will it play out in our lives?

A Place to Belong

First of all, I firmly believe that every Christian needs to have a *home church*. This will be the place where our membership is. Hopefully, it will be a place where we are known and where we have a meaningful connection. Often we may have family members who go there as well. If full-timers need a physical home base, if only a place to receive mail and register to vote, then we also need a spiritual home base to register our earthly membership in the church of Jesus Christ.

We enter the Christian life through some event that is connected with a local church. As I explained in chapter 1, I encountered Jesus Christ in the quiet solitude of a bedroom at night, but I had been highly influenced by the preaching and teaching ministry of a local church and by the personal witness of some of its members. While I haven't had any connection with this local congregation for decades, at that time I had a spiritual connection with that local church of the kind I am speaking about.

There will be many reasons that we can use to select a home church. Most of these will be personal in nature and will be as varied as we are. Presumably, there will be a similar spiritual connection that made this particular local congregation meaningful to us at the time we joined it.

Blessed are you who are able to be a member of a church in a community where you are able to spend enough time each year to be a meaningful participant in the life of that congregation. Yet to be a full-time RVer makes it physically impossible to be a part of the same local church all the time.

My life and my annual movements are probably much less varied than that of many full-timers who seek out different places to go to all the time. I have had the same summer location for the last ten years. In the same manner, I have a seasonal job in the fall that takes me to the same community each fall. Likewise, our winter location is also the same over the past few years. I do not expect much variation in this pattern in the near future. It would be easy for me to find a church in one of these regular locations with which I have a meaningful spiritual connection. This would also afford me the opportunity to connect to the spiritual and physical needs of the community through such a congregation. Ideally, this would be the best choice for a "home church," but sometimes there are other things to be considered as well. Our church membership is at present in our "home base" town, in a congregation that we attended when we lived there year-round and where several members of our family also belong. While I might like to eventually move membership to a congregation whose location was one where I could participate more regularly, this arrangement suits us for now.

You may have different reasons for belonging to your home church. The important thing is that you have such a spiritual home base. If you do not, I suggest that you establish such a relationship with a local church congregation.

Also, it is important that every believer be baptized "in the name of the Father, and of the Son, and of the Holy Spirit" (Matthew 28:19). This is an important part of Jesus' plan for us. As we have previously mentioned, there is not complete agreement among denominations and local churches as to how this should be carried out, but if you have recently become a believer and have never been baptized, you need to connect with a local church to do this.

"Home Is Where You Park It"

While we have suggested the need to have a physical "home church," as full-time RVers, we are in need of a paradigm shift when it comes to our point of view as to what exactly is our true home church. Not only RVers but all Christians could benefit from taking a look at the "big picture" here. We are all wanderers and sojourners—travelers, if you will—on this earth. It may be helpful to think at this point of the universal church as our "home church," even though everyone will have an actual local congregation to call home.

"Planted" versus "Church Hopping"

So what about all those times when you are not at the place of your home church? How do you select where you will go then?

Many of us will attempt to select a congregation by our feelings about the preacher. Certainly the man or woman in the pulpit, what they say, and how they say it will be a prominent feature by which we will judge a congregation. I would recommend, however, that you take a broader view and look at the congregation itself and how they are responding to the Lord. I will have more to say about this in the section titled "Some Practical Considerations" below.

For many of us, a lot will depend on the denominational moniker on the outside of the building. We have always been a Baptist, Methodist, Lutheran, or whatever, and that is what we will stay! If this is your attitude, I would like to encourage you to set it aside at this time. You are really missing something if you limit yourself in this fashion.

In the past twelve months, I have attended four Lutheran churches, four unaffiliated churches (including campground congregations), three Methodist churches, and two Baptist churches. I have seen the selfsame Spirit at work all across the many states of my travels and across denominational lines.

I suspect that, on occasion, God has led me into churches of various denominations simply to educate me about what He is doing in those other groups. We became full-timers because we wanted to see and experience more of our world than we could if we were "planted" in a single community. If we want to learn and grow in our life experience by being RVers, then certainly there is spiritual growth and educational value for us if the Lord leads us to visit or even to participate with denominations outside our previous experience. As we previously discussed, much is said in the New Testament about the unity of the Body of Christ. The full-time RVer is in a position to see this unity of the Body as few others are able to do.

We said earlier that the full-time RVer is the "ultimate church hopper." That was a strictly rhetorical remark. As a general rule, I do not think that church hopping is what we should be doing. Beyond the short-term educational value of visiting a few different churches, there is much more value to finding one church in a community and sticking with it throughout the duration of our stay in that community.

"Planted" Is a Relative Term?

It is very popular today to talk about being "planted" in a particular local church. Frequently you hear this term connected to these verses in Psalm 92:12-14:

> They will grow like a cedar of Lebanon;
> planted in the house of the LORD,
> they will flourish in the courts of our God.
> They will still bear fruit in old age,
> they will stay fresh and green. (Psalm 92:12-14, NIV)

Although it is a stretch from the meaning of the above scripture, the idea that is being espoused these days in the term "planted" as put forth here is that somehow believers who are in the same local congregation each week are in some way superior to those who are not.

As we have noted in previous chapters, many of us had our Christian identity wrapped up in the concept of which local church we belonged to and what we did there. If you were not a regular part of a church in the past, you probably at least viewed it as the norm for churchgoers to be involved in the same congregation regularly.

People outside the full-time RV lifestyle have difficulty understanding what our lifestyle is all about and how we manage to do some of the things we do. Our relationship to the Body of Christ is no exception to the things that contribute to their bewilderment. I have heard some people say, when I talk about my mobile lifestyle, that they don't think that they could live as I do because they would miss their home church too much. The questions, "Where do you go to church?" "How do you serve the Lord without a regular church home?" and "Who is your pastor if you have no church?" rank right up there with "How do you get your mail?" and "Where do you bank?" among the questions that I get asked.

We frequently feel guilty about this matter ourselves. It is not unusual for both full-timers and "planted" Christians to feel that if the RVers are not in the same local congregation each week, they are not living within the Lord's will. We feel guilty that we are no longer doing something that we have previously considered the right thing to do. We are in need of a new perspective about what it means to be a member of "*The* Church."

Please understand me now. I do not think you should be out here on the road as a full-time RVer or as a "snowbird" if it is not a part of God's will for your life. If the traveling lifestyle is a part of His plan, however, please understand that your guilt is ill founded and that you can be true to Him and His plans for you on the road.

Two of the books I have frequently cited in this work, *The Purpose Driven Life* and *Being the Body*, are quite clear in their opinions that being "planted" is the way to go. As I read them, I thought that the implication was clear that the authors thought that you needed to find a church and stick with it.[17]

I basically agree with this idea. We should definitely avoid "church hopping" and find a local church home to which we can commit. I think, however, that it is useful for us in the full-time lifestyle to think of "planted" as a relative term. When we are in an RV park in a community for whatever length of time, we need to find a local congregation in which to "plant" ourselves so that we

o   have a connection with the Body of Christ,
o   have a place of corporate worship and study within the fellowship of believers, and
o   have a means to connect to service opportunities within the larger community.

Then, when we move on, we will "replant" ourselves in the next community where we stop and do the same thing all over again.

I don't know about you, but I prefer not to think of myself as a tree. God made people with feet (mobility) and trees with roots (lack of mobility). Let us remember that we are not trees. The concept of being "planted" is a metaphor, and like all metaphors, it can be stretched too far to the point that it is not useful to our understanding. Paul said,

> Just as you accepted Christ Jesus as your Lord, you must continue to follow him. Let your roots grow down into him, and let your lives be built on him. (Colossians 2:6-7, NLT)

Our true roots as Christians are not primarily in a community, or even a local congregation, but in Christ Himself and in the act of *following* Him.

The very word "following" suggests movement and change, as determined by *His* will.

If we look at the "big picture" in the book of Acts, I think that what we see is a very mobile group of believers, both laypeople and those that we would have considered as "professional clergy" being moved about by the Holy Spirit and following His direction as they went. Jesus said to carry out His commission, "As you are going . . ." There can literally be no spreading of the Gospel in obedience to Jesus' commission (Matthew 28:18-20) without movement.

The early believers in Jerusalem were thriving in their faith and were growing in numbers by leaps and bounds. But they must have had a reluctance to move away from where they were until persecution scattered them to the four winds (Acts 8: 1-4). We all know the rest of the story; the scattered believers took their faith with them, and the church prospered throughout the known world because of this dispersion.

Selecting a Local Church

So how do we decide what church to attend in the community where we are staying? Once more, it is the leadership of the Holy Spirit that will be our guide. As I have traveled around, I have had no lack of a sense of the leadership of the Holy Spirit in finding a congregation to be a part of. My problem has always been not a lack of leadership but a lack of "followership."

Check out the Web Site

One thing I like to do is to check out the congregation's Web site whenever possible. Almost all of them seem to have one nowadays, regardless of the size of the congregation. What they have to say about themselves is often revealing about their values and how they understand their mission.

Many local churches have denominational affiliations that are not necessarily reflected in their names or in their listing in the Yellow Pages. This "hidden" affiliation can often be found in their doctrinal statement on their Web site.

Also, if a congregation talks a lot about their pastor and how interesting his sermons are, this raises a "red flag" for me and makes me think that their focus may be in the wrong place. Another thing that is an out-of-focus indicator for me is when I look at the church's activity calendar and see a lack of activities that would promote spiritual growth, such as Bible studies or missions involvement.

Some Practical Considerations

When all is said and done, it is the Holy Spirit who must lead us to where He wants us to be. God will bless us when we are in the center of His will. Yet there are some practical considerations about which we need to ask ourselves when we are trying to select a church:

o   Is it a part of the community in which you will be exercising your ministry to the world? This matter is discussed more fully in "The Parish Concept" below.
o   Is it a "living congregation" that is serious about representing Jesus Christ to a world in need, or does it seem like everyone is just there "putting in their time" each Sunday?
o   Is God's word truly represented in the preaching and teaching of the congregation?
o   Does it provide you with the opportunities you need for both growth and service, or if not, is there opportunity for you to take the initiative to start such an opportunity?
o   Does the congregation have a clear vision of where they are going?
o   Do you have a clear vision of how God wants you to relate to this congregation?

If the answer to any of these questions is negative, it may not necessarily mean that you should avoid that congregation, but it does mean that you have some serious praying to do. If the negative response is about the congregation itself, it is particularly important to move with caution.

On the one hand, you may be called by the Lord to have a positive influence on the situation and maybe even be instrumental in helping to turn it around.

On the other hand, if you are consistently in a church situation where you are not growing, not being fed, not able to praise and worship as you should, and the situation is consistently dragging you down rather than building you up, your inclination should be to run like the wind. If you are leaving church each Sunday hungrier for God's word and His Spirit than when you came in, it is time to ask the Lord if you are in the right place, and if not, to ask Him to guide you into a situation where you can worship Him in spirit and in truth.

The Parish Concept

An important practical consideration for selecting a local church to be a part of is what I call the "parish concept." This is related to the first item in the list of practical considerations above. For many centuries, there was only one "denomination," and most Christians likely went to the local church that was nearest to them. The greetings given by the apostles in their letters suggest in some cases that there may have been more than one local church meeting in a particular location, such as in Rome. It is doubtful, given what we know about the culture of the ancient Roman Empire that believers passed the meeting of one local church assembly on their way to another, as we do today.

In medieval times, political subdivisions and church parish boundaries were virtually identical. Even in the history of our own country, we can see this system was originally used in Virginia (Anglican) and Louisiana (Roman Catholic).

In my work as a genealogist, I learned that it was not unusual on the American frontier for families to unite with whatever church established itself nearest them in the community, regardless of what denomination they may have belonged to in their previous communities. The concepts of church and community were much more a part of one another than they are today.

Enter the automobile! Because of this invention, we enjoy a degree of mobility that is unprecedented in the first nineteen hundred years of the history of the church. It is not unusual for us to drive past several churches to get to the one of our preference. This is not necessarily a bad thing.

With our newfound mobility, however, we have sometimes lost the sense of community that was a characteristic of the parish concept. One may argue that we are perhaps simply redefining community in newer, broader terms. This may be partly true. At the same time, one of the reasons, I believe, that so many churches seem to be perplexed about how to reach out to their "community" is that their congregations often have very little representation in the geographic community in which they find themselves.

The sociological implications of all of this are something that reaches far beyond the scope of what we are discussing in this book. The point that I am trying to make, however, is that where we go to church ought to have some *strong* connection with the community of which we are a part in our everyday lives.

For many of us who are full-timers, our community will be our RV park. This is particularly true of our "destination" parks. This is why we go to these places, because they give us the communities of which we wish to be a part. For most of us, there will be one location that we like to go, usually a winter destination, because we like to be a part of the community there. I am surprised at the number of people who simply cannot conceive of the idea of going to a different park for the winter once they have found one that they like.

Many such "destination" parks offer a "church" service and, frequently, a Bible study as a part of their schedule of activities. This brings us back to the question of whether or not these "church" services are a "real church." My answer to this question is yes. In fact, what happens in these situations is probably very close to what happened in some of those esteemed New Testament churches in that a group of believers found themselves together in a locality and began meeting together to be the Body of Christ in their community.

But let us remember at this point what we said in the last chapter about "intent," that is, the intent to function as a church.

If you have been to campground worship services, you may have had the observation that I have had that many have a tendency to be somewhat ineffectual. The word "tired" seems all too often appropriate. This is, of course, an overgeneralization. I have been to some very good park services. Many that I have attended, however, seem to lack the power of the presence of the Holy Spirit that is a necessary element of a dynamic fellowship of the type of which I like to be a part.

It is usually not so much a matter of the preaching, for I have heard a lot of good sermons by dedicated and capable preachers. Nor is it a matter of the leadership of the worship service. More often, it is a matter of the congregation not responding as a congregation should. I was discussing this matter once with a fellow Gideon that I had met in the Rio Grande Valley. He said, "It's like they just come to put in their hour and that's it!"

The point here is that I feel that the congregations in these cases fail to take themselves seriously as a church. They fail to have an intent to function as a church. They look at themselves more as a "substitute church" in much the same manner that we had "substitute teachers" back in school days when our regular teachers were sick or otherwise indisposed.

There is no reason why a park congregation cannot function as a church. In fact, I have seen several that do, and that do so quite effectively. I think that our situation at Adventureland is a good example. I have also written, and will continue to write, in my blog (www.glennrivers.blogspot.com) about several others that I have attended, who take themselves seriously, and who function as a church.

One of the obstacles to park congregations taking themselves seriously is probably the transitory nature of the people involved. Many are literally "here today and gone tomorrow!" Others are around longer, but nearly all are only in the RV community for a limited time.

Another obstacle is perhaps the diversity of these congregations. Many different Christian traditions are usually represented, and they may find themselves always apprehensive about stepping on denominational toes.

There is a bright spot on the park church horizon, I am happy to say. I have become acquainted with several people who are involved with an organization known as "Christian Resort Ministries International." These folks have caught the vision and are actively involved in establishing congregations at RV parks throughout the country. One of the things that they say on their Web site is that they "bring you the Christian emphasis in a nonthreatening way." Don't think for a minute that this means a watered-down message. The Gospel and the biblical teaching is clear and unadulterated.

If your park wants to establish a park church, is in need of a chaplain, or wants to start a Bible study, contact this organization and see if they can help supply your need. Visit their Web site at www.crmintl.org for more information.

So what happens when there is no park church available or other circumstances exist that would lead you to seek a local church within the larger community? As always, the leadership of the Spirit is the preeminent factor. What application, then, does the "parish concept" have in this situation?

All of us will have a ministry to the world. We will talk about this more fully in a later chapter. Some of us will have a ministry inside the church, such as teaching, singing, ushering, etc. Almost everyone will also have a ministry outside of the church. Remember that one of the functions of the church is "equipping the Saints for the work of ministry" (Ephesians 4:12). My ministry to the world takes place outside the walls of the church, and I am very dependent on my Sunday-morning experience to be my "filling station" for the spiritual energy I need to get through the week.

As we have already noted, it is not unusual for a particular local church to have members from locations that are outside the neighborhood in which their building is located. On one occasion since we have been on the road full-time, while we were working in St. Louis, Missouri, I attended a church for a span of two months each year, in two separate years. At the time, I selected this church because some very close friends belonged there. I had thought about checking out some other churches both near our workplace and near our RV park, but for some reason, I felt led to stay at this church. The church was about twenty-five miles from where we were parking our motor home. This made for a long commute! I was delighted, however, when I realized that this church was really a meaningful part of the community to which I was ministering through my work. It was just a few miles from the store we were operating for the holidays, and several of the people who were a part of the church also shopped at the mall where our holiday store was located. This local church, though far from my "residence," ministered to me and equipped me to minister in their community. I also realized that I was spending more time in this community where I was working than I was in the community where the motor home was parked.

Similarly, I believe that there should ideally be a connection with our choice of a local church and the community that we are spending our daily lives. I could go on with numerous examples and each reader could add several more, but by now you get the idea.

Detached Believers

Perhaps one of the most important reasons why it is important to be a regular part of a local congregation is to avoid the danger of becoming a detached believer. Probably the truest statement to be found in the book *The Purpose Driven Life* is, in my opinion, the following:

> Satan loves detached believers, unplugged from the life of the Body, isolated from God's family, and unaccountable to spiritual leaders, because he knows they are defenseless and powerless against his tactics.[18]

Having been a detached believer, I experienced my descent into detachment on three levels. First, I found myself in a situation where I failed to find the support in the church where I belonged that I needed to help me get through a personal crisis that I was experiencing. Then I simply got out of the habit of going to church. Finally, I failed to see any relevance in what was going on in any of the congregations that I visited to what I was going through in my everyday life. This caused me to lack the motivation to reestablish the good habit of church attendance that I had held for so long.

Much of what happened to me was a result of my own immaturity. Perhaps something like this is what may have happened to some of you as well. Satan rarely launches a frontal attack on the immature believer. He usually is more subtle and seductive, as he was in the Garden of Eden:

Did God really say you must not? (Genesis 3:1)

Surely you will not die! (Genesis 3:4)

The enemy's most effective tactic is to convince us that the path that leads away from the one that God has set for us is an attractive path and that it can be explored as a brief adventure without peril.

Wolves and other predators are able to capture sheep by separating them from the main flock. Once separated, the sheep finds itself virtually helpless by its isolation and at the mercy of the predator. Our enemy is no less cunning and certainly no less dangerous than these.

There are many "church dropouts" in our world. The community of full-time RVers certainly has their share, if not a few more.

I believe that the greatest reason that those who come to faith in Christ later drop out of their congregations, and subsequently stay out of church, is that they come to church hungry to experience God in that special way that they can only experience in corporate worship only to walk out hungrier than when they came in. They become frustrated and think, *What's the use!*

In the past, there have been too many congregations that have taken their members for granted and have failed to help them find the spiritual resources that they needed to meet the challenges of their everyday lives.

Both *The Purpose Driven Life* and *Being the Body* gave me the impression that the authors think it is inappropriate to look at a church in terms of whether or not it meets our needs. Young believers (that is, those who are "young" in the Lord and not necessarily in their chronological age) are particularly vulnerable, however, until they have reached the level of maturity that is required to make this level of commitment. When you are thirsty, it is hard to make yourself keep going back to a dry well in search of water! I cannot escape the idea that there are individual congregations out there who either are not committed to building up the Body of their membership or are only seeking to serve a particular demographic segment among themselves.

I am particularly "uncomfortable" when I hear a congregation talk about making some certain groups of people "comfortable" (pun intended) in their church. I am all in favor of reaching out and bringing in everyone for whom Christ died. On the other hand, the Jesus I am familiar with and the Christian life I have been living all these years have been characterized (sometimes to my dismay) by having my "comfort zone" continually challenged.

We like to talk about how Jesus "changed our life," yet when we get past the initial change from darkness into light, we resist any further change. We often say at this point that "God never changes," which is certainly true. But He is in a continuous process of changing us! He remains the same "yesterday, today and forever" (Hebrews 13:8), but He is engaged in the unrelenting act of transforming us to conform to His image.

So certainly when we are trying to evaluate a local church, we need not to think of whether we are entirely comfortable there but where it will take us in our Christian growth.

I am very certain that this book will find its way into the hands of "detached" believers. In fact, I continually pray that this will happen. There are plenty of you out there who are a part of the full-time RV lifestyle who fall into this category. As we observed earlier, many have used full-timing, either consciously or subconsciously, to hide from the fellowship of believers, if not from God Himself. Some of you are wondering if you can ever have a close relationship with Christ and with fellow believers ever again and, if you do, what would it look like. Having been a detached believer at one time myself, I wrote this book with you in mind.

There are many reasons why people drop out of relationships with the local church. All seemed to be valid to you at the time. Whatever the reason, it is time to move past it. Ask yourself, "What does God want me to do now?" In fact, ask *Him* what He wants you to do now!

I would say to any of you who have been away from the fellowship of believers: ask God to lead you to the Spirit-led congregation where *He* wants you to be at each of the locations where you will spend time in your full-time RV lifestyle. There are many of them out there, and your hunger will be satisfied. You will be blessed, and they will be blessed as well for having you among them.

For all of us, whether you have become a detached believer or whether you have remained faithful in your church attendance, it is very important that we "not forsake the assembling of ourselves together" but that we seek to gather each Lord's day in fellowship with our family of faith and that we participate in the ministry of a local body of believers under the leadership of His Spirit.

CHAPTER 6

Bible Reading and Bible Study

All Scripture is given by inspiration of God and is profitable for doctrine, for reproof, for correction, for instruction in righteousness.

—2 Timothy 3:16 (NKJV)

I WROTE IN an earlier chapter that I believed that when I began to read the Bible again, it was probably the single most influential thing that God used to draw me back to Himself. For those of us who have come to Christ and have experienced the power of His Spirit, the Bible speaks in a way that no other word can speak. One of my favorite scriptures about this is found in Hebrews 4:

> For the word of God is alive and powerful. It is sharper than the sharpest two-edged sword, cutting between soul and spirit, between joint and marrow. It exposes our innermost thoughts and desires. Nothing in all creation is hidden from God. Everything is naked and exposed before his eyes, and he is the one to whom we are accountable. (12-13, NLT)

If you do nothing else as a result of reading this book, let me encourage you to start reading the Bible. God will use it to speak to you and bring you into alignment with His will and His plan for your life.

It is hard to understand how a group of writings that record God's revelation of Himself over a period of thousands of years, recorded in different foreign languages and dialects, across the lines of several cultures, and speaking to the people in the day that it was written, could actually have something to say to us in the twenty-first century. But that is the marvelous thing about the Bible. No other ancient writing or even more recent writings have a message for today like it has. And like Jesus Himself, the Bible speaks with the authority of God and not that of men (Matthew 7:29).

You will notice that I am going to avoid going into a theological discourse about the Bible and about the doctrine of God's revealing himself to us, in the way that I did with the church in chapter 3. I think that this is hardly necessary. I am presuming that all who are reading this are, at least by now, convinced that the Bible is the inspired word of God.

If you do have any doubts about the sixty-six-book Christian Bible as being the word of God, my first suggestion to you is to follow the suggestions below and start reading it. It will speak to you. I believe it was Spurgeon who said something to the effect that the Bible is "like a roaring lion. Let it out of its cage and it will defend itself!"

Also, if you doubt, or are having difficulty with the idea of the Bible as being the authoritative word of God, there are several good books that discuss this matter at length. Such a discussion is far beyond our purpose here. One of my favorite such books is Josh McDowell's *The New Evidence That Demands a Verdict*, which discusses the Bible, its God-breathed nature, and its reliability over the course of several hundred pages. McDowell also now has a new book out called *Evidence for Christianity*, which he describes as "less intimidating but still comprehensive coverage of all the best evidence for the reliability of [the Bible, and] the Christian faith."

Several books by Lee Strobel also speak to this issue. The one with which I am most familiar, *The Case for Christ*, discusses at length (among other things) the reliability of the four Gospels and the other New Testament writings as witnesses to Jesus Christ. His other books, *The Case for a Creator* and *The Case for Faith*, offer similar discussions on the Bible as it relates to those subjects.

Another timeless "classic" on this subject is *The New Testament Documents: Are They Reliable?* by the late F. F. Bruce. The author has a remarkable way of bringing out the scholarly, technical aspects of this argument in terms that most laymen can understand. This book is relatively short, yet surprisingly comprehensive.

Read one or all of the above books, but read the Bible itself at the same time. As you do, remember this: God *wants* to communicate with us! And it doesn't matter what Bible version you have in your hand. He will do so through whatever translation of the Bible we are currently using in our own language. I doubt that it ever makes much difference what translation we use when all is said and done. God will use whichever one we are comfortable with to meet us where we are and to speak to us as He wishes. Each month, in the *Gideon* magazine, there are several pages of stories written by persons who randomly picked up a Bible and, with no guidance from anyone, read a passage that changed their life.

It is no accident also that we often find whole new ways of looking at the same passages of scripture that we have been reading for years. "It is God who is at work in us both to will and to do His good pleasure" (Philippians 2:13). Sometimes it is simply time for God to reveal to us something that we were not ready to receive before. If you are new to Bible reading, don't worry much about what you don't understand. Let the part that you do understand speak to you. As time goes on, God will give you more understanding.

Get a Bible

If you don't already have a Bible, make it a priority to get one now. They sell them everywhere these days, even at Wal-Mart. It isn't important that you have a deluxe leather-bound edition. If you have a Bible already, use what you have before you decide if you want a different one. If you don't have one, just go out and buy one. Get the whole Bible if you can, or a New Testament will do for now. The important thing is to get one in your hands and start reading. There is information below that will help you to make a choice about what Bible version to get, but don't make the information grounds for indecision. If you are reading this and you don't have a Bible, finish the chapter if you must, but don't let another day go by without getting a Bible and starting a daily reading plan.

I mentioned earlier, and I say it once again, that I do not think that it matters what translation you use. God means Himself to be understood. Having studied New Testament Greek (at which I did quite well) and Hebrew (which I flunked), I think I can truthfully say that if I had never studied these languages, I would only be slightly less well off in being able to understand the Bible. Remember, it is the Holy Spirit who helps us to understand what we are reading, and He's the one who wrote it in the first place!

Having said that, I recommend that you get a modern translation. One thing that the great W. L. Muncy said over and over when I studied under him was that the Bible itself was written in the everyday language of the common man. Nobody speaks King James English as their everyday language anymore (unless you're a Shakespearian actor). There is no sense making it harder on yourself than necessary. Also, there have been several manuscript discoveries since the King James Version was first translated in 1611, and you need a Bible that takes advantage of this new knowledge. I know that there is a familiarity that we have with the KJV. Most of the scriptures that I have memorized are in that version. What we are after here, though, is understanding, and I really think that you will have an advantage if you use a modern translation. As my Gideon friend Dale says, "I like a Bible that talks like I do." Enough said about that.

Which Translation Should I Choose?

One of my teachers from the past (I can't remember which one) used to say, "All translation is, of necessity, interpretation." In other words, no matter how faithful a translator intends to be to the text that he is translating, there will come a point that they will need to interpret rather than simply translate the meaning of the text.

There are basically two philosophies that are operative in Bible translation. One emphasizes literal translation of the *words* of the text. The other emphasizes translating the *thought* of the text. Most Bible translations are, more or less, a combination of these two philosophies, emphasizing one more than the other.

If you want to understand how the translators of a particular version applied these philosophies to their work, read the preface or introduction. This should specify the way that the translators applied these principles of translation. It may also identify the translators (in most cases, there are several), briefly state their credentials and the institutions or organizations that they represent. This information should be particularly helpful to you in making your choice.

Also, there is no reason to limit yourself to just one translation. For example, while I like the New Living Translation for most purposes, I frequently use the New King James Version for Bible study, especially if I am reading or studying with Gideon friends.[19]

There are, of course, several translations out there. It would be inappropriate for me to attempt to comment on those I am not familiar with. The information below reflects only my personal experience and preference. It also mentions only translations among those that are currently popular. Here is a brief overview of the English translations of the Bible with which I am most familiar:

New Living Translation. This is my favorite translation. I am continually impressed with how very clear it makes the meaning of the text. I think that the translators have done an excellent job of remaining faithful to the original text while making it very readable. While I have heard some who have criticized it for having too simple a vocabulary, I do not see this as a drawback.

New International Version. This has become the new standard version and seems to be the most popular. If you hear someone reading from the Bible these days, or see a quotation, chances are it will be from this version. Some book publishers insist that all Bible quotations in work that they publish be from NIV. I used it for over a year but switched to NKJV then to NLT. My main dislike was that many of the familiar passages that I knew from memory in KJV were not recognizable. This was not due to a change in meaning, but the choice of words.

King James Version. This is the version that I, as well as all you other "baby boomers," most likely grew up with. Most scripture that I have memorized is from this version. While I will always have a warm spot in my heart for it, the antique English is, in my view, not only a drawback to understanding, but simply a deviation from the principle of reading the Bible in the language of the common man.

Another important thing occurs to me at this point as well. As I write this paragraph, I am doing a Bible study written by a very competent writer who chooses to use the King James Version in his studies. Also, I am attending a congregation whose pastor uses the KJV exclusively. It seems to me that much of both preaching and teaching of the Bible involve the explaining of words. While this often involves the explanation of Greek and Hebrew original words, all too often it also involves explaining the King James English words. In this book I have found it necessary to explain several Greek and Hebrew words. I shudder to think of how long this book may have been if I had had to take the time to explain numerous KJV English words as well that had lost their meaning or had taken on new and different meanings in modern English.

It is surprising in this twenty-first century how many people feel that this translation is "holier" than the other English translations. Having read the history of the translation of the KJV, I have to say with all due respect to the apparently anointed men of God who translated the KJV that there is no compelling reason to esteem them and their work above the work of those anointed Christian servants of today who are giving us translations in our own way of speaking.

Another important thing to remember is that the last revision of the KJV was made in 1762. The discovery of the Codex Sinaiticus, the oldest and considered by many to be the best complete manuscript of the Bible, was discovered in 1844-59. The Grenfell and Hunt papyri were discovered between 1895 and 1920 and are some of the oldest Bible fragments known.[20]

Most KJV Bibles have footnotes acknowledging textual differences in these newer discoveries.

I am not trying to talk against the KJV! If this is your Bible of preference, then by all means use it! I just get a little bewildered sometimes about some of the misunderstanding that exalts this version above all the others.

New King James Version. As the name suggests, this is an update of the revered King James Version. I recommend that all you King James fans give it a test-drive. It does a great job of preserving all the things we loved about KJV (except perhaps the excessive "thee," "thou," etc.) but updates the language and adds footnotes to reflect what is found in alternate Greek and Hebrew manuscripts that were not used for the original KJV. The preface to the NKJV states:

> While seeking to unveil the excellent form of the [KJV], special care has been taken in the present edition to preserve the work of *precision* which is the legacy of the 1611 translators.[21]

They have done a fine job of achieving that goal. This was my Bible of choice before I discovered the remarkable clarity of the NLT.

New American Standard Version. While I am not all that familiar with this translation just yet, I am quite familiar with the "old" American Standard Version from which it is descended. The ASV, translated by the Lockman Foundation in 1901, was W. L. Muncy's favorite version and the one he quoted (from memory) most often. He hailed it as the most accurate version ever translated into English. I had one (the 1901 edition) and used it in study for many years. I have only recently begun to acquaint myself with this new revision of this excellent translation. From what I have seen of the NASV, it is a worthy successor to its 1901 ancestor.

The Message. This is a paraphrase version (that is, more interpretation than translation) that has become extremely popular in recent years. It was translated by pastor and scholar Eugene H. Peterson. For you other "children of the '60s" it is comparable to the "Living Bible" and the J. B. Phillips translations that we knew, loved, and used in our college days. Dr. Peterson explains his own work thus:

[My] goal is not to render a word-for-word conversion of Greek into English, but rather to convert the tone, the rhythm, the events, the ideas, into the way we actually think and speak.[22]

This is an excellent rendering of Scripture, yet please remember as you use it that the interpretations are Dr. Peterson's. If you are struggling with the meaning of a passage, this version could be extremely helpful to you, but I continue to recommend that you also consult one of the more literal translations above to see something close to the actual wording of a passage.

Also, I would caution you to be careful in quoting from this version when you want to say "the Bible says . . ." While I like this version as paraphrase versions go, I cannot help but observe that, occasionally, whole sentences are added for which there is no equivalent sentence in the original text. Also, there are modern equivalent expressions added that are not supported by the meaning of the word or phrase for which they substitute. A recent reading of Acts 24 made this very obvious to me. Compare that chapter sentence-for-sentence in *The Message* with almost any other translation, and you will see what I mean.

If you find that you like more than one version, there is no law that says that you can't have more than one, although you will probably have to choose one over the other when it's time go to church or to Bible study. I currently have six different translations that I carry along with me in my motor home. I also have software versions of several more.

There is also another marvelous invention of modern publishing called a "parallel Bible." These have about four different translations in columns, side by side, making them easy to compare. I don't have any of these at present, but have had several in the past, and I liked using them. One trade-off, however, is that they tend to be very large volumes with very small print.

Study Bibles

There are several excellent study Bibles on the market. A study Bible, as you might infer from its name, is a Bible that contains numerous study aids that are designed to help you understand the Bible better and to help you find other biblical passages that relate to the one you are reading. All of the best of them contain maps, illustrations, and an incomplete (but usually adequate) concordance designed for the translation that they use.

This is where it gets a bit sticky! Not all study Bibles are available in all translations. It depends on which publisher of a study Bible has a cooperative arrangement with which publisher of a particular English version of the Bible. I have found this to be a particular dilemma because while I prefer the New Living Translation, I also prefer the study aids found in *The Nelson Study Bible* and *The Thompson-Chain Reference Bible*. Neither of these is available in the NLT.

As with the Bible versions above, these are not an exhaustive list but are the few study Bibles with which I am most familiar.

Life Application Study Bible. This Bible has good study aids that, as the name suggests, assist the student in understanding how to apply the Bible texts to one's life. The study aids are therefore less technical and more practical. The introductions to each of the books of the Bible are particularly helpful. This is a good study Bible for newcomers to the Christian faith and to Bible study. It is also good for anyone who is less interested in the technical aspects, such as word study or textual criticism, than they are in what the Bible means to their everyday lives. I particularly like the "Personality Profiles" of various persons mentioned in the Bible. There are over a hundred of them located throughout the Bible text in the places where the various persons being profiled appear.

This study Bible is available in NLT, KJV, NKJV, NASB, and NIV.

Nelson Study Bible. This is my favorite study Bible, hands down! I have nicknamed it "The Full Nelson" (and I started calling it that *before* the CBD catalog did!) because it is such a powerful study aid. The study aids are definitely traditional in their point of view, as am I. Issues of textual criticism and of difficult interpretation are tackled head-on, and usually an adequate understanding of alternate points of view are presented. I particularly like the "Wordfocus" word studies located throughout the Bible text. These give technical information about the meaning of various key words in the nearby text. There are also several "In Depth" sidebars that discuss, in greater detail, issues that are posed by the nearby text.

There has just been released a new "second edition" of this study Bible, and it is now known as the "NKJV Study Bible," and it is even better than the first edition. The new edition contains all the features of the older one, plus it adds some new features, including "Bible Times and Culture Notes," which, as the name suggests, tells about different pertinent aspects of the culture of the times that a particular Bible text is taking place.

The Nelson Study Bible and the NKJV study Bible are available in NKJV only.

Zondervan Study Bible. The study aids in this Bible are also of very good quality, though not equal to the Nelson, in my estimation. It has commentary that is similar in nature to both the Life Application and the Nelson Study Bibles, but not as comprehensive. It has a particularly good set of maps and is certainly an adequate study Bible for beginner and intermediate students. More advanced students will probably want to use one of the other study Bibles.

This study Bible is available in NASB and NIV.

Thompson Chain Reference Bible. For many years, this was regarded as the ultimate study Bible. It was the choice of many of my friends who went into the ministry. I envied them and wanted one for several years. They were also very expensive. Back in the '60s, they cost about $125 (about a week's pay for the average person back then). Modern publishing technique and probably a bit of supply and demand have brought this down considerably. I finally purchased one last summer on sale for about $40 (less than a day's pay for the average person). I was a bit disappointed. For one thing, the study aids were all contained in the back of the book rather than being incorporated in the text of the Bible, where they are in all the other study Bibles I have used. This makes one having to continually move back and forth between the Bible text and the back section when using it for study. Second, the study aids seem a bit dated and are often not as thorough as the other study Bibles.

On a positive note, the study aids in back are much like having a small Bible handbook contained in your Bible. I think that the strength of this Bible is the comprehensive way it breaks down the multitudes of topics contained in scripture and the way it organizes these topics and makes them easier to find. As the title suggests, these topics are presented as "chains" of scripture references that are linked together and can be followed link to link in the biblical text. While not as user friendly as the other study Bibles, I think that after I get acquainted with it and learn to use it, I will find this topical aspect extremely helpful to my studies in God's word.

Another very helpful feature of this Bible is the "Archaeological Supplement" in the back that lists several key locations significant to Biblical archaeology and the finds that have been made at them, including some of the more recent discoveries.

This study Bible is available in KJV, NKJV, NASB, and NIV.

Scofield Study Bible III. You who are dispensationalists will love this one as its study aids are written exclusively from that point of view and present dispensationalism[23] in the clearest manner that I am aware of. I had the "old Scofield" (which is still available) back in college days at which time it was my study Bible of choice. I have not spent time with the *Scofield III*, but it seems to have all the features of the original. The preface and the reviewers are all careful to call this an "augmentation" rather than a revision of the "old" Scofield. Apparently the *III* now comes in a red-letter edition, which the old one never did.

There were two things that I liked about my "old" Scofield that seem to still be prominent in the *III*. The chain reference system is contained within the Bible text itself and leads you through the scriptures on whatever the chain topic is. Although not as complete as the one in Thompson, the Scofield chain reference system is much more user friendly. Also, there is a date at the top of the pages within the Bible text giving the year that the events written in the text are supposedly occurring. This is, of course, based on Bishop Ussher's work. Ussher's chronology was written in the seventeenth century and has been assailed in modern times for being inaccurate, but I am smart enough to figure that the dates may be off plus or minus a few years and still find it helpful. I particularly miss the presence of the date when I read the book of Acts and am trying to figure out when the different events are happening in relation to secular history.

This study Bible is available in KJV, NKJV, NASB, and NIV.

Bible Study Aids

If you get a good study Bible, it will provide you with internal study aids that should be adequate to meet the needs of the average Bible student. When you get to be a more advanced student of the Bible, however, you will find that the helps in your study Bibles will not always be adequate to satisfy your curiosity and to help you study in the new depths in which you will want to take your studies. The following are a few of the study aids that you may want to use:

Concordances list the words in the Bible and tell you where they occur; thus, if you know a key word in a passage, you can find the passage more easily. Also, if you want to study a particular topic, you can locate the words related to that topic and look up the scripture passages where they occur. An *Exhaustive Concordance* lists every single occurrence of every single word in the Bible. If you are going to get a concordance, you might as well go all the way and get one of these. I have a *Strong's Exhaustive Concordance*, and I think it is the best, but quite technical. You almost have to be familiar with the original languages to make the best use of it. I once had a *Cruden's Complete Concordance*, and it was quite adequate for most purposes.

Bible Handbooks give a wealth of background information on the Bible itself, as well as each of the books of the Bible individually. They will be even more helpful than the material in your study Bible. They are particularly helpful in providing historical information in abbreviated but useful form. I prefer the *Halley's Bible Handbook*. Since it first came out in the 1920s, it has been faithfully updated regularly by the late author Henry Halley and, since his death, by his family. The twenty-fifth edition of this helpful book came out in 2000.

Topical Bibles, as the name suggests, list topics in the Bible and give scripture references for those topics. I had one several years ago and found it quite helpful but have not gotten to the place where I feel I need one at present. I used it mainly when I was speaking and teaching.

Bible Dictionary, Bible Encyclopedia. I find these only marginally helpful. I have a smaller Bible dictionary, which I use only occasionally. A Bible dictionary is somewhat encyclopedic in nature than what we usually think of as a dictionary. By this I mean that it goes beyond giving just the definitions for words. A Bible encyclopedia is more "encyclopedic" than a dictionary.

Commentaries contain usually line-by-line or paragraph-by-paragraph comments on the meaning of the Bible text. I once had a small collection of these but do not have any at present. They can be helpful in illuminating scripture, especially giving insight into original meaning of words or phrases. I don't find them all that helpful. They have a tendency to represent the ideas of one particular scholar or school of thought (remember what we said about "scholars" earlier). We should be most interested in what the Bible is saying to us at any given time rather than reading the opinions of what others have said. Also, these comments tend to be quite predictable after one has studied the Bible for a while. RV travelers are always conscious of weight and space considerations. I definitely do not think their usefulness is enough to justify the considerable expense and space they require.

Bible Atlases are, of course, books that contain maps of Bible lands, routes of travel of such things as Israel's wilderness wanderings, the apostle Paul's journeys, and so forth. I have always found the maps in the study Bibles and Bible handbooks to be adequate and have never felt the need to have one of these.

In addition to these, there are other more specialized study aids which you may find helpful to your needs. A trip to a Christian bookstore will usually turn up all kinds of interesting items.

Software

So you live in an RV, just like I do. Space is limited. There are weight considerations in our lifestyle as well. How do we manage to take all these *books* along with us? Fortunately, the computer age has helped us to solve this problem. Many of the Bibles, study Bibles, and study aids that we have mentioned, as well as a great many other helpful items, are available on CD-ROM and other software. We can literally carry with us a carload of Bibles and Bible study aids in this form, using only a very minute amount of space. I just saw in the Christian Book Distributors catalog that both the *Interpreter's Bible* commentary and the *Pulpit Commentary* are now available on CD-ROM. Both of these, in their printed form, are large enough to take up a shelf of their own in the average home bookcase.

I have quite a few CD-ROM software programs. I personally find two drawbacks to these media. First, the ones that I have used (and I admit that my experience is rather limited) are not what I would call "user friendly," at least to people of my skill level. Second, I have never been able to get used to the idea of "curling up with a good keyboard" (as opposed to a good book). I guess I am just behind the times, but I just can't relate to a computer screen the same way that I do to printed media. By the way, have you ever tried to "thumb through" a computer screen? So while I do find software books to be helpful regarding the saving of space and for cut-and-paste, rather than trying to copy quotations, I still carry many of the printed versions of the books we have discussed above. I like to scatter them about the motor home so my wife doesn't realize just how many I have with me.

Bible Reading Plans

I believe that everyone needs to read, at the very least, one chapter of the New Testament each day. There is absolutely nothing wrong with reading the Old Testament as well, and I really feel that we would do well to spend time reading in the Old Testament on a regular basis. I am emphasizing the reading of the New Testament as a basic minimum because you need to make it easy on yourself and not follow a Bible reading regimen that is so overwhelming that you have a tendency to skip it. Reading one chapter of the New Testament each day is something we can all find time to do. Also, if you miss a day or two and fall behind, it is not so hard to catch up.

If you are an experienced Bible reader and are very familiar with its content and are in the habit of daily Bible reading, then, by all means, stretch your comfort zone and read several chapters from both testaments. I continue to be concerned about the beginner or the person who has been away from Bible reading for a while or the person who just plain does not have the time. Better to have a small commitment that you can keep than to have a big plan that you give up on in the end. I both have experienced for myself and have seen others experience the scenario in which we undertake too ambitious a reading plan only to find it so onerous in everyday life that we simply quit. I don't want that to happen to you, especially if you are a beginner or a rebeginner in Bible reading.

Obviously, there are fewer than 365 chapters in the New Testament. This will mean that if you follow this advice, some portions will be read more than once. I saw a Bible reading plan recently that only had readings for five days a week with the suggestion that the remaining days be used to either catch up if you had fallen behind or for a more in-depth reflection of what you had read during the week. Another idea would be to use the "free" days for elective reading or to go back and ponder a chapter that you had found particularly meaningful in the past.

I have included a New Testament Bible reading plan at the end of this book (appendix 2). It is loosely based on a plan that I used many years ago when I read the Bible through for the very first time. I have made alterations in this plan according to what I thought would best serve the needs of beginning Bible readers.

The primary feature of this plan is that it does not begin at Matthew and read the four Gospels in succession. I have always thought that it is a bit redundant to read the four Gospels one after the other. I think it is more helpful to space them out over the year's reading. It also helps to keep the story of the life and teachings of Jesus fresh in your mind. At the beginning of the plan, I have outlined the arrangement of the books and the basic ideas by which I have chosen that arrangement. We will suffice to say here that the arrangement is somewhat chronological and also somewhat by author or other general grouping.

If you don't like my plan, or you feel you want something different in approach, there are many others out there. *Discipleship Journal* (www.discipleshipjournal.com) has three very good ones on their Web site. I saw a plan recently that a friend of mine was using that tried to present the whole Bible chronologically from Genesis through Revelation. It was September before the reader got to the New Testament! I don't recommend doing something like this until you have otherwise read through the Bible at least three times.

Just Do It!

So enough advice already! Get a Bible and start reading. Decide on a time that you can devote to Bible reading each day. If you and your spouse want to read it together, so much the better. Just be sure that one doesn't hold the other back. Have a plan for one to go ahead alone if the other cannot make the designated time or if both cannot make an adjustment in their schedule to read at the same time. It might be a good practice in such a case for one to go ahead, and then both read again together when time permits. Just don't hold each other back. Encourage each other instead.

Perhaps you are like me and your schedule varies according to where you are and what you are doing. If I am working, I am more likely to be working a variety of hours. This makes it tough to read the Bible at the same time every day. If I am working a late shift, I have my time with the Lord, including my Bible reading time, later than if I work an early shift, but I have resolved to have it early in my day. This makes the whole day go better for me. If I have early commitments and cannot do this, I like to have my Bible reading anyway, and then look at the same passage again if I have to postpone my prayer time until later. We will talk about the relationship of the Bible reading to prayer more fully in the next chapter. Just remember that there is no law against reading more than once a day.

Sometimes too, it is good to discuss your reading with a Christian friend. If both of you are reading the same thing, you can hold each other accountable to be faithful in your reading habit. The book of Proverbs says,

> As iron sharpens iron, so a friend sharpens a friend.
> (Proverbs 27:17, NLT)

Bible Study

Bible *reading* and Bible *study* are two qualitatively different things. The goal of Bible reading is just to read the word and let God speak to you through it. The goal of Bible study is to get a more in-depth understanding of an entire portion of scripture. Everyone should be engaged in Bible study all the time. Whether it is in a Sunday school setting, a Bible study sponsored by either your local church or in your RV park, or whether you are studying on your own, it is a good idea to be engaged in a weekly study of God's word. I really have a tendency to slack off at this point. The park where I spent the last two winters has a weekly Bible study, but I convinced myself that I needed to spend the time writing. I always regret these decisions afterward.

A group Bible study has the advantage of having people of differing levels of spiritual growth. Some members will often have insights that will be helpful to the other members. A downside is that there are sometimes persons in the group that will like to monopolize the discussion with their own ego trips. A good leader will know how, or will learn how, to manage these.

Joining a Bible study with others tends to be like going to a church full of strangers (see chapter 5) except that you can be sure that the group will be small enough that you won't have the opportunity to "blend in with the woodwork." That can make it even more difficult at first, if you're bashful like me, to try to get started. As with church, it is usually worth the effort. If it turns out not to be something that builds you up, you can always drop out.

At Adventureland in the summer, we have three to four small-group Bible studies going on at the same time within the Workamper community there. Bible studies that meet in an RV tend to be small and quite intimate. These groups tend to be extremely worthwhile. Also, the "iron sharpening" factor mentioned above is intensified when the groups are this small. If you are ever parked somewhere for a month or more and have the opportunity to be a part of or even start a small group, it would be well worth your while. I wouldn't worry too much about the qualifications of a group leader. Often God is able to speak to people who are open to His Spirit and honest about His word, regardless of the qualifications of any of the participants.

If you cannot or do not care to be a part of a group Bible study, it is always an option to study by yourself. There are many Bible study guides that you can use to assist you. There will be several available at Family Christian Stores or other Christian bookstores. An organization known as the Navigators is another source of Bible study materials. Check out their Web site (www.navpress.com) to see what they have to offer. Many commercial study materials do not offer very much commentary. They are more likely to be aimed at guiding you through your own study of the word than telling you what to think. I see this as a positive factor rather than a negative one.

How to Study the Bible

Whether you are studying on your own or with a group, whether you use prepared study guides or you study unaided, here are some principles of how to go about studying the Bible. As often before, most of my remarks are tailored to beginners and rebeginners. Those who are well experienced in Bible study probably have already established good study habits by now. Some of the methods mentioned will be based on those I learned when I was regularly doing Navigators Bible studies.

First, pick out the section of the Bible that you wish to study. I suggest studying a book at a time. Don't do topical studies unless you are more familiar with the Bible or have a good knowledgeable leader. I have always found the letters of Paul the easiest to study simply because he had a way of making himself understood. The Gospel of John is also a good starting point.

Study the book of the Bible the same way it was written, line by line, paragraph by paragraph, and thought by thought. The writers wrote a paragraph at a time, and when you study it a paragraph at a time, there is less danger of taking a passage out of context.

1. Start by reading the larger context—a section of the book that contains two or three or more chapters that talk about the same subject or time period. For some of the smaller books of the Bible, this will mean reading the entire book. Then go back and read the first paragraph on which you are focusing your study.
2. Rewrite the passage in your own words.

3. Ask and answer the following questions:

    - What is the most important idea or ideas expressed by the passage?
    - What questions are raised in your mind by the passage?
    - What are some possible answers to these questions?
    - What does the passage say to me?
    - How can I apply this to my life?

And then there comes that inevitable dilemma. What happens when you find yourself responding negatively or even outright rejecting what seems to be the obvious truth that the passage seems to be saying? Sometimes there is a problem of interpretation. We do not understand what God was trying to say to the original audience. The meaning seems to have been obscured by millennia of cultural history that we do not understand. But is that really the case? Ask yourself this question: "Why am I responding this way?" Is it misinterpretation, or is it that we just don't want to make the paradigm shift in our thinking and our behavior that the passage requires of us?

Many people find it easy to see what a passage of scripture says to someone else. It is harder to see what a passage should mean to you. Prayerfully ask the Lord to reveal your innermost need and to make it clear what He is trying to say to you. It is your growth and your relationship with the Lord that is important here.

Move at Your Own Pace

Sometimes it seems that a course of Bible study is going too fast for you. If you are studying on your own, take your time. If you are studying with a group and it goes too fast for you, do your own study after the group is done, using the method above, paragraph by paragraph. So what if it takes you a year to get through the book of Romans or the Gospel of John or whatever. After all, we invented the clock and the calendar. God's perspective is eternity.

Whatever you do, be sure that you commit yourself to the daily reading of God's word. If you are not already engaged in daily Bible reading, begin today. Begin, in fact, at this very moment. The time you spend will be an investment in your Christian growth that will pay dividends far beyond what you can ever imagine.

CHAPTER 7

Prayer

Very early in the morning, while it was still dark, Jesus got up, left
the house and went off to a solitary place, where he prayed.
—Mark 1:35 (NIV)

I REGARD MY own prayer life to be yet in its infancy or, at best, some very primary stage, so I will have little wisdom to offer here regarding how to pray. I am persuaded, however, by what little wisdom I have that it is not so important *how* we pray as it is that we do pray. If we approach God with a sincere heart, He will indeed meet us. James assures us,

Draw close to God, and God will draw close to you. (James 4:8, NLT)

In the end, that is what prayer is all about—drawing close to the Master of the universe and cultivating and enjoying our relationship with Him.

As we will discuss later in this chapter, the disciples asked Jesus, "Teach us to pray," and teach them He did. He will also teach us to pray if we ask Him.

Personal Prayer

There are, in fact, many types of prayer. There is, of course, public prayer, in which we pray before a group of people. There is corporate prayer, which differs from public prayer in that the person who is praying aloud is taking upon themselves the role of a leader and the people are praying with that leader. There is the prayer we say before a meal. There are the prayers we pray at our family devotional time. All these are important, and there are probably other types of prayer that I have not mentioned. What I want us to focus on in this chapter is *personal* prayer, that is, your own one-on-one time with the Lord. This is the type of prayer that is the foundation of all the other kinds of prayer.

Your personal prayer life is a direct outgrowth of your personal relationship with Christ. A Lord and Savior who is unapproachable and incommunicable would be unthinkable! God desires, above all else, to have a relationship with us. Christ came to restore the relationship with God and to restore our approach to and consequently our communication with God.

> According to his eternal purpose which he accomplished in Christ Jesus our Lord. In him and through faith in him we may approach God with freedom and confidence. (Ephesians 3:11-12, NIV)

If you pray with a prayer group, this is great. If you pray with your family, this also is a good thing. Each of us, however, needs his own personal time with the Lord. This needs to be yours and His time together and that alone. If you and your spouse have a meaningful prayer time together, this is a marvelous blessing, but it does not replace time by yourself with Him.

When I came back to the Lord after my "wandering period," it was almost like starting over again. I had memories of a great prayer life, particularly back in those "good old" college days. But I am learning some new attitudes this time around and the days ahead promise to be even brighter than those in the past.

Is It a Formula or a Relationship?

We are probably all familiar with the often-used scripture in Revelation, made even more well-known by the painting that depicts Jesus knocking at a door:

> Here I am! I stand at the door and knock. If anyone hears my voice and opens the door, I will come in and eat with him, and he with me. (Revelation 3:20, NIV)

We usually use this verse to illustrate Christ offering salvation to the lost, which, in fact, He does in a similar way. In reality, though, this particular verse is addressed to believers with whom Jesus wants to renew an intimate relationship. It is His desire to have fellowship with us.

The new buzzword nowadays is "relational prayer." In other words, the emphasis is on establishing a relationship with our Lord and growing in that relationship through our prayer life. Yet many times we are, instead, trying to find a method or formula that we can follow. If we will just ask in the right way, we reason, God will give us the desires of our heart. In other words, we are often looking for a way to manipulate God into giving us whatever it is that we want.

An author with whom I am acquainted wrote a book called *Seven Steps to Effective Prayer*. I was unable to see a copy, so I don't know what the seven steps were, but a great deal of the literature that is written about prayer presents some similar kind of formula. If we will just do this and this and this (and perhaps this), God will answer our prayers. Much that passes for prayer consists either of just flat-out telling God what to do or of an attempt to go through the right formula or ritual that God will find pleasing enough that He will be persuaded to answer us as *we* see fit. These formulas are an attempt to find "the right combination" that will unlock the heart of God. We think that surely there must be a "key" that, if we only will learn to use it, will result in answered prayer every time. This is the way that we have learned to view prayer. This is the point of view of the natural man.

As far as I am concerned, there are only two "steps" involved in prayer. First, take time to talk to God. Second, take time to listen to Him.

Conversational Prayer

Jesus' disciples asked Him, "Lord, teach us to pray" (Luke 11:1). In Luke's version, what followed was what we call the "Lord's Prayer" or the "model prayer," which nearly everyone in our culture, both Christian and non-Christian alike, can recite by heart. Within the church, we have dissected it and examined its parts and have proceeded to turn it into yet another formula for convincing God to give us what we want.

I suspect that the disciples learned more about prayer from watching Jesus' prayer habits than from His verbal teaching. In our text passage above (Mark 1:35), Jesus got up early in the morning and went off to "a solitary place" to spend time with His Father. You can be sure that their conversation went beyond the "model prayer"! In fact, that word, "conversation," is probably the most apt description of what I picture as what went on when Jesus withdrew to prayer. I picture these times that Jesus withdrew to be with His Father as a two-way conversation that came out of the relationship He had with the Father that He loved so dearly and who so dearly loved Him.

I was first introduced to the concept of "conversational prayer" when I was in college. Several other students and I met after school for what we called "prayer lab," which was simply a collegiate metaphor for what we were doing. We met in a small room on one or two days a week, after classes had ended for the day. We closed the blinds so that we could shut out the distractions of the world outside and had just enough light to read the Bible when we wanted. Then we just had a conversation with the Lord and among ourselves and related what we felt God was speaking to us about as individuals and as a group. You would think that this would turn into a free-for-all or would have been seen by some as an opportunity to "preach" at the rest of the group. Surprisingly (or perhaps not so surprisingly), we were very much of one accord, and it was an experience of remarkable spiritual growth for all of us.

I think that we had an unoccupied chair for Jesus to "sit" in, which helped us to focus on the fact that He was indeed present. I still use that technique today. I focus on Christ's presence with me by envisioning Him sitting in one of the seats in my motor home. I am not trying to limit Him, but am attempting to help *myself* focus on His presence.

Listening and Petitioning

The word "conversation" is different from "petition." It suggests a two-way exchange. Listening is the part of conversational prayer that distinguishes it from other ways to pray. Jesus said, "My sheep hear my voice, and know me" (John 10:27). Learning to listen for His voice and distinguishing it from all the other inner voices that each of us has crying for our attention is a vital part of our spiritual growth.

Nearly every book of the Bible either contains or mentions prayer. For instance, the Psalms, while they are a collection of songs, also contain examples of prayers. If you look particularly at the Psalms of David and see the friend-to-friend intimacy that they frequently convey, it is easy to see why God referred to David as a "man after my own heart" (Acts 13:22).

Many of the prayers of individuals that are recorded in the Bible are what we would call "petitions," that is, they were asking God for something or calling for His intervention and help in some circumstance. Much of what we do that we call prayer is the offering up of our petitions. There is nothing wrong with petitioning God. In fact, this is a *part* of what we should be doing. Two significant scriptures stand out that deal with petitioning:

> Do not be anxious about anything, but in everything, by prayer and petition, with thanksgiving, present your requests to God. (Philippians 4:6, NIV)

> Give all your worries and cares to God, for he cares about what happens to you. (1 Peter 5:7, NLT)

Listening for God's answering voice is also something that we find frequently in scripture. Two significant examples come to mind. First, there is Elijah, who was fleeing into the wilderness to escape death at the hands of Jezebel. The story is recorded in 1 Kings 19 and is very much a *dialogue* between him and the Lord.

Another story is that of the prophet Habakkuk, who makes his petition to the Lord and then says,

> I will climb up to my watchtower, and stand at my guardpost. There I will wait to see what the Lord says, and how he will answer my complaint. (Habakkuk 2:1, NLT)

The thing that has always struck me about this passage is that Habakkuk, after his petition had been made, waited to *hear* an answer from God. He expected this to be a two-way conversation.

In the New Testament, there are many examples as well. One in particular is found in Acts 10. Peter was up on the rooftop deck at a friend's house, praying. It does not say what he was praying about. This is irrelevant to the story. God spoke to Peter in a vision, and Peter was listening. After the vision was given, the scripture records,

> Meanwhile, as Peter was puzzling over the vision, the Holy Spirit said to him, "Three men have come looking for you. Go down and go with them without hesitation. All is well, for I have sent them." Acts 10:19-20, NLT)

The men, of course, had been sent by a God-fearing Roman officer named Cornelius, who himself was responding to an answer to his prayers that he had likewise received in a vision.

The point for us here is that God speaks to us in prayer. There is a long history of it. The Lord God invited His prophet Jeremiah even as He invites us, His people of today,

> Call to Me, and I will answer you, and show you great and mighty things, which you do not know. (Jeremiah 33:3, NKJV)

Keeping a Prayer Journal

I use a prayer journal. I recommend their use to everyone. I have been keeping a prayer journal since 2003. Notice that I did not say "regularly" or "faithfully." I do keep it, more or less, every day now, but it was one of those habits that was hard to cultivate, and easy to lose.

Keeping a prayer journal is good for me because it helps me to keep my prayers focused. Perhaps you will not have as much trouble staying focused as I do, but I think you will be blessed nonetheless as you record what goes on in your prayer time.

One thing I can see, obviously, is how my prayers have been answered. Another thing is that I often see patterns emerging as to what I am concerned about and what the Lord is saying to me about things I need to do.

I find that when I am traveling, it is harder to keep the journal. Also, when I have arrived at a new destination, sometimes it takes a couple days before I can reestablish my routine. Sometimes there are other reasons that the prayer journal gets put aside for a while.

I have also noticed that, occasionally, the prayer journal itself becomes the focus of my daily prayer time and therefore becomes an obstruction rather than a help. There also are the times that I lay the prayer journal aside for a while. The focus needs to be on Jesus and hearing his voice. The journal, after all, is just a tool to use to help rather than hinder my prayer life.

You will probably need to develop your own routine for your daily fellowship time with the Lord, but here is what I do and how the prayer journal helps.

First, I read my daily scripture passage. Then I select a portion of it that means something special to me at the time. I then write out this passage by hand in my journal. Writing it out helps me to explore it more fully. Writing each word just seems to drive the passage home and make me more conscious of everything about it. After this, I write something about why the passage is special to me. I always write in my journal as though I am talking directly to the Lord, which in fact, I am. I approach this portion of the process similarly to what I would do if I were writing a letter to Him.

At this point, I pause to try to listen to what the Holy Spirit is saying to me. If I feel that there is something specific that God is trying to tell me, I write it down. If I feel led to another scripture, I go to it and meditate on it for a while, writing it down too if it seems necessary.

If I am burdened with something, or if there is a pressing concern, which there usually is, I write this out, telling the Lord what I am feeling and pouring my heart out before Him. Then again I write out what I may feel He is saying to me.

Often, as I am having this time with Him, I feel led to pray about someone or something. I always write these things down, as I often later see why I was led to pray about something in this way or at that particular time.

At the end of the journal entry, I note and pray for some of the items from the daily prayer calendars. I am a Gideon, and we have prayer calendars for nearly everything. I am particularly earnest to pray for a list of young men and women whom I have met while participating in the Bible distributions at the Military Entrance Processing Center. I also think it is very important for us to take time to pray for situations that are outside our everyday experience, as well as praying for our friends and family and acquaintances.

Every few weeks or so, I go back and read what I have written. As I have gone back over my journals from time to time, I can see where the Lord is clearly at work in my prayers. I also see where some of those other voices have had their say. I can truthfully say that, as time has gone on, I have found that I am getting better at hearing the Lord's voice than I was in the beginning.

A prayer journal needs to be private. If there is ever a part of it that you want to share with someone else, copy it and show that part to them. It is extremely important to protect the privacy of your prayer journal. It is just between you and the Lord. It is essential that you feel free to write anything in it, even your ugliest thoughts. You simply cannot be this free in your expression if *anyone* has access to it besides yourself. Also, in the same spirit, avoid the temptation of peeking in your spouse's journal.

The Prayers of the Holy Spirit

Just recently, through the help of one of my brothers in the Lord who is a part of a Bible study group that I have been facilitating, I have rediscovered the importance of the following passage of scripture:

> And the Holy Spirit helps us in our distress. For we don't even know what we should pray for, nor how we should pray. But the Holy Spirit prays for us with groanings that cannot be expressed in words. And the Father who knows all hearts knows what the Spirit is saying, for the Spirit pleads for us believers in harmony with God's own will. (Romans 8:26-27, NLT)

This passage reminds us that, even though we have free access to God through Jesus Christ, we often do not know either what to pray for or how to pray for something. The Holy Spirit, however, intercedes for us and closes this spiritual gap. My friend told several times about how he simply asked the Spirit to pray for him about certain matters about which he had no idea how to pray. I tried this too, and I got some impressive answers, which were certainly not the answers I would have thought of or would have asked for myself. We may not have need for an earthly priest, but our heavenly High Priest (see Hebrews 4:14-10:22) is just exactly who we need.

A Picture Is Worth a Thousand Words

Somehow, over the years, I have gotten hung up on the idea that I had to articulate every word of my conversation with God when I prayed. In recent years, I have realized that I can also pray in pictures. That is, I can picture in my mind what I want things to look like and just lift up that picture to God. Likewise, I have learned that I can pray whole thoughts without uttering in my mind every word, as I am doing now when I write, for instance. Our Lord knows our thoughts and can read our minds, and it is not necessary to articulate every word of a prayer thought to Him.

Intercession

In both our private prayer life and our prayers with others, an important dimension for us to include is intercession. Intercession is, of course, praying for others.

One of the most famous intercessory prayers in the Bible is the prayer of Jesus as recorded in John 17, in which Jesus offers a final intercession before His betrayal. He offers this prayer on behalf of not only His disciples but for "all who will ever believe in me through their message" (John 17:20).

Another famous intercession is Abraham's intercession for Sodom and Gomorrah in Genesis 18. Abraham tries to strike a bargain with God, first getting Him to agree to spare the cities if there were fifty righteous persons there. He then "bargains" God all the way down to His agreeing to spare them if there are only as few as ten righteous persons there, which, of course, there were not.

This begs the age-old question of whether or not God's mind and plan can be changed by prayer. In his book *Prayer: Does It Make Any Difference?* Philip Yancey has a very good discussion of just this issue. I recommend that you read it if you want to know more about this, as he discusses this subject with greater insight and expertise than I am able to do. In this book, he cites the example of C. S. Lewis comparing the answer to this question to a stage play.[24]

When I began to study the craft of writing, I was surprised to learn that, for many novelists and playwrights, in fact for the best of them, the actions of the characters are not entirely decided in advance. The author decides on the theme of the story and the general plot, the personalities and life stories of the characters, and perhaps a general outline, and then simply lets the characters interact in his imagination along those lines, making up the details as he goes. Does God, the master playwright, perhaps do the same thing?

As I stated at the beginning of this chapter, I am, to say the least, uninformed and inexperienced at what makes prayer work. What I do know is that repeatedly we are told in scripture that we need to bring our requests and petitions before God and to intercede in prayer for others.

Intercession as a Ministry

The more I read about intercessory prayer in the scriptures and the more I hear testimonies and see prayer at work in the lives of Christian "prayer warriors," the more I am convinced that intercessory prayer is a ministry that all of us are called to perform. I am also convinced that some are called to be intercessors as their main, regular ministry. As we will discuss in a later chapter, everyone has a ministry that God lays upon their hearts to perform. Some brothers and sisters, I believe, have a heart to pray and to intercede for individuals and groups and situations. While this ministry may occur in private, it is a valid, necessary, and biblical ministry.

Seeing Things God's Way

One of the essential aspects of communicating with God is to find out what is on His mind. We often think of prayer as trying to change His mind, but to the contrary, it is a time to change our minds to more closely reflect that which is consistent with His will and His plan. God wants to show us His master plan for the universe and His will about what part we will play in that plan.

Consider this scripture:

> And we can be confident that he will listen to us whenever we ask him for anything *in line with his will.* And if we know he is listening when we make our requests, we can be sure that he will give us what we ask for. (1 John 5:14-15, NLT; emphasis added)

Old Testament and New Testament Prayer

In the Old Testament, people most often prayed for deliverance from their individual circumstances, or for God to act in their present moments. In the New Testament, and particularly in the prayers of Jesus, there is a broader perspective than just the immediate. Here we find, in addition to prayers for their immediate circumstances, people also praying in a way that looks ahead to God's greater plan beyond immediate circumstances. Jesus prayed:

Thy Kingdom come. Thy will be done on earth as it is in heaven. (Matthew 6:10, KJV)

We too need to remember to pray in light of the goal of the Great Commission (Matthew 28:19-20) and in light of the ultimate victory and the coming Kingdom of our King of Kings and Lord of Lords rather than just in light of our immediate concerns.

Spending Time with God

Luke records that on the night before Jesus chose the twelve, He "went to a mountain to pray, and he prayed to God all night" (Luke 6:12, NLT).

You need to have an adequate amount of time to devote to your personal prayer time as well. As I read about many of the "giants" of the faith, I am impressed that many of them spend several hours in prayer on a regular basis. In our text passage at the beginning of this chapter, it does not say exactly how much time Jesus spent, but I have always gotten the impression that there were multiple hours involved. We should plan on no less than an hour to be spent with the Lord each day. There is, by the way, no law that says that we can only have one prayer time a day.

At this point, I have another one of those confessions to make. I do not spend a full hour or more in prayer *every day*. This could explain why I am not a spiritual giant like those who do. I have come to a point, however, that I am so blessed and my prayer time is so enjoyable to me that I do spend that amount of time more often than not. But there are always things that get in the way for me. I'm sure that there are for you as well. If for some reason you cannot take a full hour on a particular day, don't put it off to another day. It is more important to have your time with Him each day than that you have the full hour or more. By the way, aren't you glad that He always has time for us!

Spending a Day in Prayer

Several years ago, I designated an entire day that I spent in prayer. At the time, I had a major life decision that I needed to make, and this was the main impetus behind my doing this. I had read *How to Spend a Day in Prayer* by Navigators founder, Lorne Sanny (recently back in print in the Navigators' *Nav Classic* series) and went by the guidelines therein. I don't remember what all it said. I do remember packing my Bible and a lunch in a backpack and heading out to a county park in a quiet spot. I also remember that it was a very rewarding experience. I don't think it takes either a lot of imagination or a book to tell you how to do this.

It has been over forty years since I did this. In this day and age, it is hard to imagine spending a whole day doing any one thing. I still hold on to the idea that one day I will do this again. In retrospect, I wish I had done this in conjunction with many of the other major life decisions that I have had to make in the last forty years.

Prayer Retreats

Often, there is the opportunity that presents itself for us to engage in a formal, organized prayer retreat. This is a designated time to go to a specific place with a specific group of people and perhaps listen to some inspirational messages and to spend a significant amount of time in prayer. It is not necessary, however, to go to such an organized event to have a prayer retreat. Often, we can have our own personal or family prayer retreat. Like the day-in-prayer above, we can simply select a time, and "just do it."

The theme for the January/February 2007 issue of *Pray!* magazine was "Prayer immersion: Purposeful retreats into God's presence." You can view a copy of this issue online at *www.praymag.com* (*Pray!* magazine is no longer being published). One of the writers talked about what he called "floor retreats" where he got down onto the floor of his home and stayed there as long as he felt God leading him to stay. The article is titled "A Place of Transformation." I recommend this issue if you want either information or inspiration about prayer retreats of both the organized and the informal variety.

Practice of the Presence of God

A book that has been read by many and has been very popular among Christians for over three hundred years is *The Practice of the Presence of God* by Brother Lawrence.[25] I tried to read it, finally, a couple of years back, but lost interest about a third of the way through. Written in about 1692, its tone and point of view were a bit too "catholicy" for me. I think that the basic thesis of the book makes an important point, however. We have a tendency to look at prayer as something confined to a particular place (church or the dinner table, etc.) or time. *The Practice of the Presence of God* puts forth the idea that God is everywhere, and rather than *going into* His presence at a particular place and time, we are in fact in His presence at all times. *The Practice of the Presence of God* is about the practical realization and recognition of this fact and about a continual dialogue with the Lord as we are going about our daily tasks. As David observed,

> I can never escape from your Spirit!
> I can never get away from your presence! (Psalm 139:7, NLT)

Indeed, we do need to both recognize and take advantage of the fact that God is with us through the presence of His Holy Spirit wherever we are 24/7! To realize that He is beside me and I can talk to Him, or just realize His presence when I'm climbing the leg of that one-hundred-foot Ferris wheel, changing light bulbs, is both awesome and comforting.

Another time that I find it significant to "practice the presence of God" is when I'm driving down the highway in my motor home. Sometimes listening to Christian music is a help. Other times it is better to silence all but the noise of the open road. In this way, our RV can become a house of worship.

A very real part of our personal prayer life is to know and to practice the fact that we can go to Him at any time and at any place, not just at those times and in those places that are set aside for the purpose of prayer.

Some Further Advice from Jesus

Jesus gave some additional advice to us regarding prayer and how to go about it:

And now about prayer. When you pray, don't be like the hypocrites who love to pray publicly on street corners and in the synagogues where everyone can see them. I assure you, that is all the reward they will ever get. But when you pray, go away by yourself, shut the door behind you, and pray to your Father secretly. Then your

Father, who knows all secrets, will reward you. "When you pray, don't babble on and on as people of other religions do. They think their prayers are answered only by repeating their words again and again. Don't be like them, because your Father knows exactly what you need even before you ask him! (Matthew 6:5-8, NLT)

Three things stand out for me in this passage:

1. Prayer is to be directed toward God, and not intended to be a show that we put on in front of men.
2. Don't babble on by repeating the same things over and over again. God heard you the first time.
3. God, in His omnipotent concern for our well-being, already knows (and by implication, is willing to grant) our every need.

What Do We Really Need from God?

Here is yet another variation of that persistent, burning question again. If God knows everything and knows what we need before we ask and if God's will is perfect, why should we pray? This idea, in fact, controlled my prayer life during much of my life and certainly throughout the "wandering period." I have come to discover in recent years, however, that I come to God in prayer not so much because I need *things* from God or because I need God to change things but because I need *my Father*. It is the act of coming to God, of spending time with Him, of learning of His will and His plans for us, of just resting in Him that is what we should seek for our prayer life to be about. Like all relationships, our relationship with God is one that should be enjoyed as an end in itself, rather than a means to an end.

An Act of Faith

Another important thing to realize is that prayer is an act of faith, and this very act of faith is, in itself, pleasing to God. We pray about something because we believe that God can and will answer us. We affirm by prayer our belief that God exists and that He has the power, the will, and the intention to do what is required to bring about the outcome for which we pray. This is especially true when we pray for others. This is what the author of Hebrews is expressing to us by the Holy Spirit when he writes,

And it is impossible to please God without faith. Anyone who wants to come to him must believe that God exists and that he rewards those who sincerely seek him. (Hebrews 11:6, NLT)

So come to Jesus. Ask Him to teach you to pray. Speak to Him in the private space of your life. Learn to listen for His voice. Follow Him as He intended for you to do. Most importantly, abide in Him and learn to love and enjoy the privilege of spending time with Him. As is so often the case with scripture, James hits the nail on the head when he says,

The earnest prayer of a righteous person has great power and produces wonderful results. (James 5:16, NLT)

CHAPTER 8

Christian Literature

Fix your thoughts on what is true and honorable and right. Think about things that are pure and lovely and admirable. Think about things that are excellent and worthy of praise.

—Philippians 4:8 (NLT)

I AM SURPRISED at how few people read regularly. Moreover, I am surprised that among those who do, how few read anything of substance. As I look back, I realize that I have been an avid reader all my life. Reading has been one of my great joys, and despite some who say that it is not a worthwhile pastime, what could be better than the learning that can result from time spent reading the printed (or electronic) page?

The late Earl Nightingale, as well as the multitudes of motivational speakers in the generation that followed his footsteps, has driven home the theme "We become what we think about." This is the same idea that Paul puts forth in the scripture text above. There are many things that we can fill our minds with in our multimedia culture. If we think about the good things and if we fill our minds with the things of God, we will nourish our souls and will reinforce all we have gained through our reading of God's word and prayer. I believe that we should all be engaged with Christian literature on some level in our lives at all times.

Devotional Literature

One way that we can be engaged with Christian literature is through the use of devotional books and magazines in our daily prayer and Bible reading time.

There is a great deal of devotional literature available to every believer. I know many who are not particularly avid readers who, nonetheless, find the use of a daily devotional guide a great help in their prayer life. These usually consist of a single-page entry with a Bible verse, a thought for the day centered on that verse, and a prayer suggestion. These are intended to help the reader focus on a particular Biblical truth and to help apply that truth to their life. You will note a similarity between this and how I mentioned in the last chapter that I used my prayer journal.

I have used devotional literature often in my life in the Lord. I am not currently using any. This is not to say that I never will again. I simply realized that I had grown to the point that I felt like I needed to structure my own devotionals.

One form in which devotional literature is available is in small monthly and quarterly magazines, many of which are sponsored by the major denominations and are readily available, usually free of charge in most churches' literature racks. There are also independent magazines that are available by subscription, such as *Guideposts* and *Our Daily Bread*. One of the best ones I have seen recently is called *On the Right Note*, and it is published by K-Love Radio and distributed free to their financial supporters. Go to www.klove.com for more information.

There are also many very good devotional books available at most Christian bookstores. Most of these bookstores have a separate section for them. These vary from 30 days of daily devotionals to up to 366 days. It is this author's intent, by the way, to produce a 366-day devotional book as a follow-up to this book that will tailor the daily thought in such a way as to be more of interest to RVers.

There are also several online devotionals available. I have many friends who use these rather than the printed variety. As I have said previously, I haven't quite warmed up to the computer screen as a reading medium, at least not to the point that I can substitute the electronic page comfortably for the written page. As a result, I don't use online devotionals very often.

In any case, the use of devotional literature can be of great benefit in planting "seed thoughts" for your prayer time. I frequently hear my friends tell me how their daily devotional was just what they needed for what they were facing that particular day.

Christian Periodicals

There are a great many Christian magazines in the world today. Some are quite good and many also not so good. Most major denominations publish at least one, if not several. These usually feature articles on Christian living and commentary on the news of the day. The articles are presented in a way that is fresh and up-to-date. They are also short. So if you don't care for a steady diet of reading, you can get in a few minutes what you might take hours to get from a book, although not as great in depth and detail. And when you are through with them, you can usually take them to the laundry room or the recreation hall of your campground so that others can benefit from them too.

A downside for us RVers, of course, is the expense of mailing them. You will have to have them sent out from your mail service, and there is a consequent added cost in this. I have my third-class mail sent out to me monthly, and sometimes that means that my magazines are almost a month old by the time I get them. Often, I have the mailing addresses changed to where I am if I am going to be in the same place for a while. If you do this, be sure to change the addresses back well before you leave the area. Many times it takes a period of ten days or more for the magazine to process the change of address.

Some periodicals that I have subscribed to in recent years that I have found helpful include *Charisma*, *Discipleship Journal*, *New Man*, *Christianity Today* and *Pray!*.

Christian Books

I think that everyone who is literate should be reading a Christian nonfiction book at all times. I frequently have two or three that I am reading at any given time. Reading books on prayer, prophecy, or theology, to name a few subjects, or about any aspect of Christian living that you may be interested in, can help you be more informed about that subject.

We all need to read things that challenge our thinking. I wonder if a part of why so many individual Christians, as well as many local congregations, seem stale and stagnant is because these folks never stimulate their minds with fresh ideas through the reading of these types of books. Just think back to all the action that was generated by the book *The Purpose Driven Life* a few years ago. I have often said that the main effect of that book was not that it taught us anything new but that it opened up dialogue and discussion and challenged many people's comfort zones.

There are many Christian bookstores in most communities where Christian books can be found. The small independent bookstore is alive and well still in the Kingdom of God. There are also large franchises. My favorite is Family Christian Store. Cokesbury is another good one. The latter tends to have in stock many of the theology and church history titles that others seem not to have as often. Many denominations have their own bookstores, such as Baptist Book Store (SBC) and Concordia Books (Missouri Synod Lutheran).

I don't necessarily recommend buying Christian books at the secular bookstores such as Barnes & Noble or Borders. They identify as "Christian" any book that remotely deals with Christian subject matter, including those that revile the name of our Savior or that do not recognize Him as we do. Unless you are familiar with an author or book by name, you are buying the proverbial "pig in a poke" when you shop at one of these.

Online bookstores include Christian Book Distributors, who offer most books at good discounts. There are many books that CBD sells that are not readily available elsewhere. If you are shopping online for a particular book, I suggest that you try here first. Another source of good Christian books, both fiction and nonfiction, is Crossings Book Club. Log on to www.crossings.com for more information. Amazon.com now has what they call an online "Christian Bookstore" as a part of their book-selling operation. This is of the same basic philosophy as what we said about the secular bookstores above. They also host an online "Christian" book forum, which has some interesting reading, but is hardly deserving of the label "Christian" in my opinion. Amazon can also be a good source for out-of-print books.

By the way, thanks for choosing to read this book.

Christian Fiction

I do not read very much fiction. My wife, however, simply *devours* it! I have a hard time getting interested in fiction books. There seems to me to be too much interesting nonfiction and so much to learn from it that there is little time left for what seems to me to be reading for entertainment. I have had a couple of fiction books on my nightstand for about two years. Both are well written by well-known Christian authors, and I have read only a few chapters in both. I intend to read them all the way through "someday."

It is clear to me that I am in the minority at this point, however. The genre of Christian fiction and particularly romantic novels have literally exploded in recent years. And why not? If you are going to read a novel, why not read a Christian novel? I am not saying that everything we read has to be "Christian," but think back to what we said at the beginning of this chapter about what we fill our minds with. While I admit once again that I have not spent much time reading novels in recent years, I think that even a cursory look at what is out there in the secular world will show that much of it is just plain trash. Even the well-written novels, such as the *Da Vinci Code*, seek to purposely distort the Christian worldview and distort fact and discredit the Christian faith. The Christian novel offers us an alternative to these distortions.

So go visit that Christian bookstore and let's get reading. Reading of Christian literature is a road to understanding what is going on in the greater Christian community. We often get quite provincial in our thinking and in our outlook on life. Reading can help us to broaden our horizons regarding what is happening in the greater Body of Christ.

Often we are unable to actually hear from such Christian leaders as Max Lucado and Beth Moore, except through their writing ministries. Reading can give us access to so many of these whom Christ has used to bless so many lives.

Your growth in grace and knowledge of the Lord will certainly be enhanced by your reading.

CHAPTER 9

Praise

Praise the Lord, all you nations. Praise him, all you people of the earth. For he loves us with unfailing love; the Lord's faithfulness endures forever.

Praise the Lord!

—Psalm 117 (NLT)

IT MAY SEEM strange to you that I would devote an entire chapter to praise. It would seem by definition that praise would be a part of either our prayer life or our worship experience in the local church, so why deal with it here, in a separate chapter?

Let me tell you what happened to me. I grew up and in fact spent most of my life in church environments that emphasized the "Message." That is, the preached word, the sermon, and the Bible text that it was based upon were the center of worship. Everything revolved around the message and its delivery. Any type of praising our Lord was something coincidental.

When I found my way back to the Lord, following my wandering period, I was highly influenced by what is nowadays called "praise and worship music." I am not trying to suggest that participating in this style of music is the only way to praise the Lord. I am saying that what I found was that over about a half century of living, I had a whole lot of praise bottled up inside me! When I began to express this part of my worship experience, I found this marvelous release of all these feelings of praise. It was something I needed very much. It is something I find hard to fully express with words.

Another thing that happened to me at this time was that, through this experience, I began to realize that the message was an important *part* of worship. The reading of the word and the proclamation of the word are a fundamental part, but they are in fact only a part of what the corporate worship experience should be. Praise is an essential element of our worship as well.

The word "praise," or some form of it, is used over two hundred times in the Psalms alone. Since the Psalms were Israel's songbook, it is obvious that the act of praise was an important part of their worship to God. It should be no less so for us.

Praise does not have to take the form of music. It does not need to be only something that is done only in corporate worship. Like worship itself, it can take place in any setting. One can be alone or be with others who can join in.

While I do not think it is necessary to discuss the subject of praise and why we should do it at length, I did find a few interesting items as I was reading through the scriptures regarding it.

Praise as a Sacrifice

In the book of Hebrews, after discussing the sufficiency of the sacrifice of Christ on the cross, the writer makes this statement:

> With Jesus's help, let us continually offer our sacrifice of praise to God by proclaiming the glory of his name. Don't forget to do good and to share what you have with those in need, for such sacrifices are very pleasing to God. (Hebrews 13:15, NLT)

By saying this, the author of Hebrews tells us that now it is praise that we are to offer up as a sacrifice rather than the old animal sacrifices. I had always thought of this in the past as a metaphoric sacrifice. However, the book of Hebrews is all about the superiority of the sacrifice of Christ and the "better" way of the New Covenant. Praise, then, is a better offering of sacrifice that can and should be offered up in thanksgiving for what Christ has done. It is listed in equality with doing good and caring for those in need, saying "such sacrifices are very pleasing to God."

A similar sentiment is expressed by the prophet Hosea:

> Bring your petitions, and return to the Lord. Say to him, "Forgive all our sins and graciously receive us, so that we may offer you the sacrifice of praise." (Hosea 14:2, NLT)

Praise, then, can be an offering, and it is an offering that we can all afford.

The Environment Created by Praise

David declared in the famous messianic psalm,

> But thou art holy, O thou that inhabitest the praises of Israel.
> (Psalm 22:3, KJV)

That use of the word "inhabit" is a peculiar one, but it is certainly the most literal.[26] The New King James Version and the NLT use the word "enthroned." The idea of the word thus translated gives the idea of a king that sits on a throne in the midst of his subjects. The idea that I think that this phrase is trying to put forth is that praise creates an environment in which the presence of God will be manifested.

There is a marvelous story in 2 Chronicles 5 about what happened when the Israelites performed the worship service to dedicate the first temple, the Temple of Solomon. All the people of Israel were gathered. All the animal sacrifices had been made. All the priests and Levites, whether on duty for the day or not, were gathered. All the singers and musicians were dressed in their finest and assembled in the praise band. Then the scripture records,

> The trumpeters and singers performed together in unison to praise
> and give thanks to the Lord. Accompanied by trumpets, cymbals,
> and other instruments, they raised their voices and praised the
> Lord with these words:
>
> "He is so good!
>
> His faithful love endures forever!"
>
> At that moment a cloud filled the Temple of the Lord. The priests
> could not continue their work because the glorious presence of the
> Lord filled the Temple of God. (2 Chronicles 5:13-14, NLT)

This mighty shout of praise created an environment in which God manifested Himself in such a powerful way that the priests could not even go on with what they were doing! I have been in a few praise situations, both public and private, where I would not have been surprised if something like this would have happened.

Praise as a Weapon

Many of us are aware of Paul's passage in Ephesians 6:10-17 about the "whole armor of God" to be used in our spiritual warfare, but the Bible shows us that praise can be a weapon too.

Another story from 2 Chronicles tells us,

> After consulting the leaders of the people, the king appointed singers to walk ahead of the army, singing to the Lord and praising him for his holy splendor. This is what they sang:
>
> "Give thanks to the Lord; his faithful love endures forever!"
>
> At the moment they began to sing and give praise, the Lord caused the armies of Ammon, Moab, and Mount Seir to start fighting among themselves. (2 Chronicles 20: 21-22, NLT)

You can read for yourself how successful this tactic was for them. There were other instances of this happening as well. The point here is not that we should send singers before the troops going to battle, praising the Lord (although perhaps that may be a good idea), but that in our own spiritual warfare, if we send out our praise, we have this one more weapon in our arsenal to help us win.

So then, praise is something that should always be a part of our experience in our relationship with our God. If we use it, we benefit in ways that go far beyond just expressing our love and gratitude to Him. If we neglect to offer praise, we do so to our own detriment. Let us join with the psalmist and

> Praise the Lord!
> How good to sing praises to our God!
> How delightful and how fitting! (Psalm 147:1, NLT)

CHAPTER 10

Stewardship:
Part A, Whole-life Stewardship

What do you have that God hasn't given you? And if everything
you have is from God, why boast as though it were not a gift?
—1 Corinthians 4:7

M Y FRIEND BOBBY Shomo likes to point out in his stewardship
sermon series this simple foundational truth: "Everything belongs
to God."[27] The clear teaching of the Bible is that we are but managers of
that which He has entrusted to us. The meaning of the word "steward,"
as used in the Bible, is "manager."[28] Our text verse above tells us this very
same thing.

I have mentioned several times throughout the course of this book that
I had the good fortune to have studied under the great Dr. W. L. Muncy.
The theme of Christian stewardship was one that Dr. Muncy had not only
studied in-depth but one for which God had placed a special burden on
his heart to teach to anyone who would hear. Dr. Muncy also conducted
"Stewardship Revivals," in much the same manner as an evangelistic
campaign, in local churches.

Dr. Muncy "wrote the book" on Christian stewardship. To my
knowledge, he was the only person to author a book solely on the subject
of Christian stewardship in his generation. Only recently have I seen
another book written on the subject. Dr. Muncy's book *Fellowship with God
Through Christian Stewardship* is still available through Amazon.com through
Kessinger Publishing. I am indebted, in the comments that follow, to that
classic volume of literature. I am also indebted to his influence during the
many hours I spent listening to Dr. Muncy in both my home church, where
he came frequently as a guest speaker, and in the classroom during my time
as a student at what is now Missouri Baptist University.

This is not to say that all the comments that follow are a recap of Dr.
Muncy's ideas. First of all, I do not agree with everything that he has to say.

Second, a lot of the information in his book is somewhat dated. He wrote at the time of my parents' generation, and many of the ideas, including some of the economic paradigms and assumptions of those former generations, are not appropriate for today's economy. Also, I have picked up a few ideas of my own along the way.

Stewardship as a Whole-life Concept

We need to see stewardship, first of all, as a whole-life concept. Traditionally, when we think of stewardship, we usually think of giving a *portion* of our money. Sometimes we carry the concept a bit farther and see it as giving a *portion* of our time or a *portion* of our talent back to the Lord. But there is a larger concept here that we need to see. *Everything* belongs to God! Every aspect of our lives is something that rightfully belongs to Him. We have been appointed by Him to be His *managers* of all things that He has entrusted to us.

Managers

Stewardship, by dictionary definition, is about the management of the resources of another, *to whom we are responsible*, rather than our ownership of resources, and their consequent use. As we have already pointed out above, the word for "steward" in the KJV, from which we coined our term "stewardship," is translated as "manager" in the newer translations. A manager is, of course, not the owner.

In our lead verse above, Paul is reminding the Corinthians that everything they have has been given them by God. It is interesting to note that this is one of the earliest books in the Bible that talks about spiritual "gifts." Paul offers this verse in context of the Gospel ministry that had been entrusted to him. It is difficult to talk about biblical stewardship outside the context of whole-life stewardship. He also said earlier in the same paragraph,

> Moreover, it is required in stewards that one be found faithful.
> (1 Corinthians 4:2, NKJV)

Paul was saying this in the context of his being a steward of "the mysteries of God," but he said it in such a way as to take an example from stewards in general. It was a "no-brainer" in that day, as it should be in ours, that a person who was a steward was expected to perform his duties faithfully.

He Owns Everything—Even Us!

I never thought much about this before, but as I was rereading Dr. Muncy's book in preparation for this chapter, I came across this statement:

> This trust [which God has placed with us] includes much more than material things because God owns *persons*, as well as possessions; and He has intrusted [sic] men with the use of time, personality, opportunity, and material things.[29] (emphasis added)

It is repulsive to the modern ear to talk of human beings as being owned by anyone. Indeed, for us to own our fellow men is a despicable practice that largely has been, and rightfully should be, wiped from the face of the earth. Yet God is our Creator and consequently owns us. We like to think of ourselves as "free moral agents" and as our own man or woman, but the truth is, if we are reconciled to Him, we are His. As Paul put it,

> You do not belong to yourself, for God bought you with a high price. (1 Corinthians 6:19-20, NLT)

This gives us a whole new perspective on another passage about giving:

> For I can testify that they gave not only what they could afford, but far more. And they did it of their own free will. They begged us again and again for the privilege of sharing in the gift for the believers in Jerusalem. They even did more than we had hoped, *for their first action was to give themselves to the Lord* and to us, just as God wanted them to do. (2 Corinthians 8:3-5, NLT; emphasis added)

It is not my intent in the foregoing comments to take away from the fact that we submitted to Christ of our own free will. Neither do I intend to diminish the fact that we are now adopted sons and daughters of God, through our relationship with Jesus Christ. I do, however, wish to point out that God has a rightful claim on our lives and how we conduct ourselves as we live them. Our adoption by Him is a relationship that is bestowed by Him as His free gift to us. We are to recognize this claim that He has on us as the foundation of our faithful stewardship of all else with which He has entrusted us.

The Psalmist admonishes us,

> Come, let us worship and bow down, Let us kneel before the LORD our Maker; For he is our God, *And we are the people of His pasture, and the sheep of His hand.* (Psalm 95:6-7, NASV; emphasis added)

Talent, Time, and Opportunity

I remember one year at my home church in St. Louis, we had our annual stewardship (read "fund-raising") campaign that sought to emphasize, in a way, this whole-life aspect of stewardship. I don't remember if it was convention-wide or just our congregation, but the campaign was accompanied by a jingle. This catchy little jingle was sung to the tune of "The Battle Hymn of the Republic." I can't remember the verses, but the chorus went like this:

> Talent, time, and opportunity,
> Talent, time, and opportunity,
> Talent, time, and opportunity,
> We give it all to Thee!

I mention this here only because I am hoping that this little song will stick in your mind as it has in mine all these years, and it will help you remember this discussion of stewardship as something that involves our whole lives. Let's talk about a few of these areas of stewardship.

Decisions about Life

Such important decisions in life as our choices regarding marriage, our pursuit of education, choices of career, when to retire, and where to live are just leading examples of life choices in which we rightfully submit to the Holy Spirit's leadership as the proper stewardship of our lives. Small decisions too should seek to honor God. I'm not saying that whether we take a right-hand turn or a left-hand turn should always become a matter of prayer or anything like that. I am simply trying to get across the point that we need to be concerned about the decisions we make if we want to be good stewards of the opportunities God gives us.

The Use of Time

Stewardship in the use of our time does not necessarily mean that we should always be engaged in "Christian" activities. I do enjoy these and probably spend more time at them than many folks do. I find in them opportunities for greater spiritual growth. However, there is nothing wrong with being a sports fan or a boating enthusiast, a hunter, a sport fisherman, or any number of other things. In fact, these activities are where we can engage the world for Christ and show them what it means to be a Christian. Once again, honoring God with our use of time and submitting to His will in our selection process of how we use our time is a part of our whole-life Christian stewardship.

Personality

We often see how much we are all alike that we fail to see the differences and the uniqueness that we each possess. We mentioned earlier that God is responsible for forming us all into the people who are uniquely suited for the tasks that He has for us to do. That is not to say that He is responsible for all the rotten things that seem to happen to most of us, but that He is able to use them to make us what He wants us to be. Our personality, therefore, is numbered among those things that He has placed in our trust to be used for His honor and glory. We will discuss this more in-depth in the chapter on ministry. For now, let us suffice to say that using (and improving) our personality that the Lord has given us is a reasonable part of our stewardship.

How Wealth Is Created

We often have the idea in the back of our subconscious minds that the creation of wealth is inherently evil. This is not the case. At the risk of sounding like one of the modern-day "prosperity preachers," which I am not, I would remind that it is not the creation of wealth that is evil but the love of it and the improper use of it that is taught against in scripture.

The nation of Israel was warned by Moses during his address to them in Deuteronomy to not get too self-confident when they became prosperous in days ahead and had built themselves comfortable homes and had enjoyed the success of prosperous crops and herds. He reminded them of their history and of what the Lord Jehovah had done for them and their ancestors, and he reminded them:

> You may say to yourself, "My power and the strength of my hands have produced this wealth for me." But remember the LORD your God, for it is he who gives you the ability to produce wealth. (Deuteronomy 8:17-18, NIV)

Wealth must be produced with God's leadership, that is, by pursuing occupations, investments, and business endeavors that He directs us to do. It will be a result of our following God's plan for our lives, not our own doing.

To get back to our original foundation for stewardship, "Everything belongs to God." Yet sadly, as we look around us, I don't think one has to be a person of particularly great insight to realize that much of the world's wealth is in the control of those who do not belong to Him. Additionally, much of the activity that is creating new wealth in our world is also in the hands of unbelievers. Consequently, I have often thought that the reclaiming by Christians of our Father's wealth is an inherently positive activity.

Let us remember at this point that one of Jesus' two famous parables about good stewards, the one we also refer to as the "parable of the talents" (Matthew 25:14-30; Luke 19:11-27) involves the creation of wealth. In this parable, it was the amounts by which wealth was increased that determined whether the stewards were good or bad at their stewardship.

Could you imagine what the world would be like if all of the "Forbes 500" were committed Christians who were creating wealth, and then using their wealth at the Holy Spirit's direction, for the glory of God? It staggers my imagination when I think of it! Granted, most (probably all) of those who read this will not be among that elite number of wealthy people. I have never encountered a Forbes 500 member out on the road. Yet my point is this: true biblical stewardship involves the possibility of creating wealth. A true Christian steward will create wealth at God's direction by means that will honor Him; then that true steward will use that wealth for the honor and glory of the Lord Jesus Christ and the furtherance of the Gospel.

How We Earn Our Money

An important outgrowth from the idea of Christian stewardship in the creation of wealth that we need to mention separately is that how we earn our money is important. Whether we are wealth creators or simply wage earners, the choice of how we earn our money is an important question. There are legends that I have heard, about gangsters during the "Roaring Twenties" who gave generously of their illegally obtained funds to the church. If this were true, certainly this would be an example of improper giving, and such funds would be considered unfit to be received by the Body of Christ.

While this is an extreme example, we all earn money in some way. As full-time RVers, we all have pensions, retirement funds, savings and investment proceeds, wages earned as "Workampers," or all or any combination of the above. Have we sought the will of God in our choice of work? Have we sought His advice in our choice of investments?

In chapter 2 we quoted the scripture:

> Since we are living by the Spirit, let us follow the Spirit's leading in every part of our lives. (Galatians 5:25, NLT)

Are we following the Spirit's leading in the matter of how we earn our living? We will expand on the theme of our choices of work in a later chapter, but for now this is a valid question to ask ourselves in regard to our Christian stewardship.

Stewardship of Our Bodies

There are many ways that we can abuse our physical bodies. These include, but are not limited to, substance abuse, improper diet, failure to properly care for our health, failure to exercise, endangerment by acts of recklessness, failure to acknowledge physical limitations, and many more. Unfortunately, for many of us, by the time we get to be seniors, we have established a long history of these abuses and have formed habits that are difficult to break.

It is hard not to be judgmental as we look around us and see the shape that some of us have gotten ourselves into. While none of us seniors are in as good a shape as we once were, that's really not the point. Some of our peers are the living epitome of the old cliché "If I had known I would live this long, I would have taken better care of myself."

Obesity has been called an epidemic in our society. Much of our social lives revolve around food. Winter Texans in the Rio Grande Valley often joke about consuming meals at two-hour intervals. The truth is that most of us are paying too much attention to calorie intake and not enough to calorie output. This seems to this casual observer to be the leading cause of obesity among RVers. This is a shame, as most of us have the time for long, brisk walks these days.

Many of us are not obese but cannot walk a hundred yards without gasping for breath or being in such pain that we have to stop. If we are otherwise physically fit, it would not be impossible for us each to increase our walking distance by a hundred yards per day until we could finally be able to walk a respectable distance.

Sometimes our physical condition is in an irreversible state, yet nearly all of us can be in better shape than we are. There is no excuse for most of us to remaining in the shape we are in. We can start where we are and gradually get to a better place physically.

Let us heed these words of Paul:

> [Our bodies] were made for the Lord, and the Lord cares about our bodies. And God will raise us from the dead by his power, just as he raised our Lord from the dead.
>
> Don't you realize that your bodies are actually parts of Christ? (1 Corinthians 6:13-15, NLT)

Paul is talking here about abusing our bodies by means of sexual immorality, which is certainly applicable to our discussion here as well, but I would like us to see a less specific level of application here. Sexual immorality is certainly one way that we can abuse our bodies, but it is not the only way, and if our bodies belong to the Lord, any abuse of them is inconsistent with good stewardship.

While our bodies are a temporary dwelling for our use here on earth, there is a connection that they have with our eventual eternal spiritual, resurrection bodies, and they deserve to be respected accordingly.

Our present bodies have been given us by God for our use here on earth, and we need them to be at the highest level that we can make them function so that we can fulfill the purpose that He has for us. We already have enough things that hold us back. If our body holds us back as well, we owe it to ourselves, as well as to our Lord, to do all within our power and through His power to better our condition. Good stewardship demands for us to care for our bodies as well as we can so that we can prevent or minimize the extent to which we are held back by our physical bodies.

I don't think that it is necessary for us to spend a lot of time in the gym or get into marathons or Senior Olympics (though I wouldn't discourage these things), but we need to be good stewards of our physical bodies, whatever that may mean for each of us.

In the beginning part of this chapter, we quoted a part of the following passage, which I now quote in its entirety. Again, Paul is speaking in the context of sexual immorality, but let us see a broader meaning here:

> Don't you realize that your body is the temple of the Holy Spirit, who lives in you and was given to you by God? You do not belong to yourself, for God bought you with a high price. So you must honor God with your body. (1 Corinthians 6:19-20, NLT)

The Planet

Finally, in regard to the concept of whole-life stewardship, we must address our stewardship regarding how we treat this planet, Earth, which is entrusted to us. As full-time RV dwellers, we spend a greater amount of time in touch with the environment than do many or our non-RV peers. Most RV parks in which we find ourselves staying take steps, to a greater or lesser degree, to enhance the natural environment in which they are located. Many of us selected the RV lifestyle because we wanted to be more in touch with nature. Often, our leisure time is spent in outdoor pursuits and in exploring the natural world. It should be clear to us that we need to be good stewards of the environment that has also been placed in our trust. Genesis 1:28 reads,

> Then God blessed them and said, "Be fruitful and multiply. Fill the earth and govern it. Reign over the fish in the sea, the birds in the sky, and all the animals that scurry along the ground." (Genesis 1:28, NLT)

This is not to be seen as a license to abuse or destroy but a responsibility to protect and to maximize the best possible uses of the earth that God intended.

It is not only those who are in touch with the outdoors that have a responsibility to the environment. All persons living on the earth leave a "footprint" on its face. We RVers are often taken to task by others for the amounts of fuel that we use, yet it is a known fact that need not be argued here that our RV rigs use less energy over all and release fewer pollutants into the environment than the average site-built house. Yet this fact does not absolve us from thinking about what we are doing and employing the responsibility of good stewardship to our choices that affect the environment.

Despite the alarmist rhetoric that we hear about so often these days, I do not believe that we are capable of completely destroying the planet. This old world was here for a very long time before any of us got here, and I believe that it will remain, and human life will remain on it for as long as God purposes for it to be so. I do, however, believe that we are capable of making wrong choices that could make our planet a less pleasant and more dangerous place to live. We who are "going forth in the Name" should be leading the way toward good stewardship of our environment.

So now we see that stewardship is greater than just the giving back to God a portion of our money, as we have often been accustomed to thinking. It is first and foremost a concept of recognizing that *everything* belongs to God and that we have been appointed managers of all he possesses and has placed in our trust.

Some, in an attempt to grasp this concept of whole-life concept, have also lost sight of the fact that stewardship does, in fact, include giving of the monetary funds in our possession to the work of Christ in the world. Often, Dr. Muncy used the term "partnering" with God by funding endeavors that we cannot carry out ourselves. Most specifically this includes funding the work of the local church, the greater denominational efforts, missionary activities, hospitals, schools, and the like. It is this aspect of Christian stewardship to which we now turn our attention.

CHAPTER 11

Stewardship:
Part B, Giving Tithes and Offerings

> Each man should give what he has decided in his heart to give, not
> reluctantly or under compulsion, for God loves a cheerful giver.
> —2 Corinthians 9:7 (NIV)

NOW THAT WE have seen that Christian stewardship, in its
entirety, is a concept that involves every aspect of our lives, let us
focus on that important (and sometimes sensitive) aspect of stewardship
that involves the giving of our money.

Stewardship and Fund-raising

As we said at the close of the last chapter, the act of giving, raising funds
to advance the cause of Christ, and to pay the bills in the local churches and
other ministries is an important part of Christian stewardship and is the
action with which we most often associate the word "stewardship."

Whenever we speak of stewardship campaigns in our churches, it usually
involves the task of fund-raising. Stewardship campaigns usually center on
the rather unbecoming task of asking (begging?) for funds and pledges of
funds for the support of a local congregation or some other Christian cause or
organization. Often, stewardship campaigns in local churches involve trying
to convince their members to be 10 percent (or more) givers, commonly
referred to as "tithers." The local churches have a long history of protecting
the tithe as their divine right of entitlement.

For those of us out here on the road, and often for our more stationary
brethren as well, there are two main questions as to the giving of our wealth
back to the Lord as tithes and offerings: How much should we give? And
to whom?

How Much Should We Give?

I believe that there is one basic, overriding principle regarding the amount that we should give. It is expressed in our text scripture above. Some of the other translations substitute the word "purposed" for the word "decided." I like the word "purposed" in this instance, as it suggests, to me anyway, a sense of commitment. I think that the Lord is asking us, first of all, to make a commitment to giving. I think also that this verse makes it clear that it is to be a commitment from our own free will, with no coercion except that from His Holy Spirit.

I am not even going to get into the argument of the tithe. If a tenth of your income is what you purpose in your heart to give, so be it. You are to be admired because many do not give this much. I read a survey recently that indicated, as many other such surveys have in the past, that the average church member gives 2 to 3 percent of their income to their local congregation.

Well, now it's time for another one of those confessions again. I am not a 10 percent giver either. I was once, for several years. In fact, for one year, I was a 15 percent giver. But I also had, at that time, what I have come to see as a bad attitude. I was very legalistic about the whole matter. The tithe was a command that I felt I had to obey. I disobeyed the text verse above in that I gave out of a perceived necessity, and somewhat grudgingly too, I might add.

To add to that bad attitude, I also had a bad attitude of giving in expectation of the perceived reward that I would get in return. After all, the area of tithing is perhaps the only place that God invites us to put Him to the test:

> "Bring the whole tithe into the storehouse, that there may be food in my house. Test me in this," says the LORD Almighty, "and see if I will not throw open the floodgates of heaven and pour out so much blessing that you will not have room enough for it. I will prevent pests from devouring your crops, and the vines in your fields will not cast their fruit," says the LORD Almighty." Then all the nations will call you blessed, for yours will be a delightful land," says the LORD Almighty." (Malachi 3:10-12, NIV)

I certainly was not the "cheerful giver" that the Corinthian passage says that the Lord loves! It didn't work out for me, and I didn't have the maturity at that time to understand that the Lord had a greater lesson that he wanted to teach me in all this, so I gave up the practice.

W. L. Muncy and others often point out that the practice of giving the tithe precedes the Mosaic Law, and therefore is an "eternal principle."[30] I have no argument with this idea. I aspire to being a 10 percent (or better) giver once again in the future, even as I aspire to be a 10 percent (or better) saver in the future, albeit for different reasons. Oddly, I save about the same percentage that I give. Is there a message in that for me? I find my "natural man" resisting this idea. God will show me in His own good time. I'm a slow learner sometimes.

A wise man, who was conducting one of those local church stewardship campaigns, told me once that if you cannot give 10 percent, decide on a percentage that you are comfortable in giving and commit to that amount with the idea of increasing the percentage as the Lord prospers you and as you get your financial house in order. "As a man purposes in his heart, so let him give."

I do not give in the 10 percent range at the present time because I have done some really stupid things with money, and I have a lot of commitments to creditors. This is certainly not the Lord's fault, but I feel that He understands and He accepts that which I am able to give and honors my commitment to get this financial house of mine in order and to do better in the future as I seek His guidance in my financial life. There is yet another statement that is made by Paul about giving that I really had never noticed before, until recently:

> Give in proportion to what you have. Whatever you give is acceptable if you give it eagerly. And give according to what you have, not what you don't have. Of course, I don't mean your giving should make life easy for others and hard for yourselves. I only mean that there should be some equality. (2 Corinthians 8:11-13, NLT)

I have never heard that message proclaimed from the pulpit! I really think that this passage gives us a true picture of what the giving of our money is all about. Giving eagerly in proportion to what you have. Sometimes what we have or do not have to give is a result of other stewardship decisions we have made regarding how we spend our money.

When it comes to us who are RVers, one only has to look around an RV park to see a wide range of financial capabilities. I have often observed, when looking at one of those six-figure motor homes, that for what one of those costs, I could pay mine off and still have enough left to comfortably supplement my pension for the remainder of my life. Now I'm not begrudging anyone their nice motor home but just trying to point out a stewardship decision. I am sure that God is happy to bless us all with a nice RV rig, but there is always a decision as to whether we are being good stewards in these choices we make.

So now that we are drawing closer to the Lord and desiring to be good stewards of that which He has entrusted to us, let us seek His guidance in how we spend as well as how we give.

If I have an objection to the idea of the tithe, it is because it is a legalistic concept. In this way, it seems to me to be antithetical to the way of the New Testament. Muncy and others often like to point out that the tithe, while not commanded, is "implied" in the New Testament. Once again, I have no argument with that teaching. What strikes me, however, as I read the pages of the New Testament, is that teaching of the tithe is conspicuous by its absence. In all the passages that we have looked at regarding giving from Paul and others, the word "tithe" is not mentioned. There are only two passages of the entire New Testament that use the word "tithe." One is the seventh chapter of Hebrews, where the writer discusses the historical event of the giving of a tithe from Abraham to Melchizedek. The purpose of the passage is to demonstrate the superiority of the priesthood of Melchizedek over that of the Levites and, consequently, the superiority of Christ over them both. The other, more significant passage is from Jesus Himself:

> What sorrow awaits you Pharisees! For you are careful to tithe even the tiniest income from your herb gardens, but you ignore justice and the love of God. You should tithe, yes, but do not neglect the more important things. (Luke 11:42, NLT)

While this passage is often used to point out that Jesus approved the practice of tithing, it is clear, in addition, that He is pointing out to the "tithers" that there are indeed more important things for our consideration.

The absence of a discussion and of specific instruction about tithing leads me to believe that there must be a more important principle of giving taught in the New Testament. Let us consider this passage for a moment:

> All the believers were one in heart and mind. No one claimed that any of his possessions was his own, but they shared everything they had. (Acts 4:32, NIV)

Back in the '60s and '70s, that passage was seen by a lot of folks as a license to go and start up "Christian communes" where everybody pooled their money and all lived together in one place and so forth. It didn't work out so well for them. Most of them that I am aware of failed. I'm not so sure that it worked out so well in ancient Jerusalem either. Paul was always collecting money for the "the poor among the saints in Jerusalem" (Romans 15:26). I'm not really sure why the believers in Jerusalem had such a problem with poverty. It didn't seem to be an issue so much with the rest of the New Testament churches. As we suspected, however, there are a couple of larger principles involved here.

First, there is a recognition that all of their wealth belonged to the Lord. Second, there is no limit that was placed on how much or how little they gave. They literally gave it all to the cause of Christ! Finally, their giving was based on the needs that they observed within their community.

And what a difference this was between the Christians and the world in which they lived. I am sure that the culture around them was certainly like our own. The "me and mine first" attitude that is so representative of human nature was certainly the leading attitude in their culture. These disciples were truly transformed in their attitudes toward their money. They went from the natural tendency toward stinginess to the more Christlike attitude of generosity.

Many years later, John would put it this way:

> We know what real love is because Jesus gave up his life for us.
> So we also ought to give up our lives for our brothers and sisters.
> If someone has enough money to live well and sees a brother or
> sister in need but shows no compassion—how can God's love be
> in that person? (1 John 3:16-17, NLT)

Good question! Jesus tried to teach us the same lesson in the parable of the Good Samaritan, found in Luke 10:25-37. Since this story seems to be so well-known, even among unbelievers, it is hardly necessary to quote it here.

As always, I don't pretend to have all the answers about all this. The Lord still has much to teach me, and as I have observed earlier, I tend to be a slow learner in this particular area. I think it is safe to say, however, that it is a definite teaching in the New Testament that giving must

o   be a purposeful commitment,
o   be from a willing heart,
o   be according to what we have, rather than what we don't have,
o   have no upper or lower limits, and
o   be based on the needs that exist and on the Holy Spirit's direction as to how we should go about fulfilling those needs.

That leads us into our discussion of the next important question:

To Whom Should We Give?

There is a long history in the Bible of the practice of supporting those who have been set apart by the Lord to minister to us. Paul gives us a quick but concise overview of this practice when he says,

> Don't you realize that those who work in the temple get their meals from the offerings brought to the temple? And those who serve at the altar get a share of the sacrificial offerings. In the same way, the Lord ordered that those who preach the Good News should be supported by those who benefit from it. (1 Corinthians 9:13-14, NLT)

In the Old Testament, the tithes and the offerings were considered by the Israelites as being given to the Lord as an act of worship. The priests and Levites, however, were to be able to partake, with little restriction, of the leftovers from the acts of sacrifice. Paul tells us here that the Lord had revealed to him that the same thing is to happen to those who give their full time to the ministry of proclaiming the Good News. He continually had to make the point to the Corinthians that he voluntarily gave up that right and earned his own living so that he would not present a "stumbling block" to them. Many today who minister to the needs of the RV community have made a similar decision to support themselves and their ministry so that the Gospel will go forth unhindered. Yet there are many more who deserve and should receive our support so that they will be free to meet our spiritual needs. As Paul wrote to Timothy,

> Elders who do their work well should be respected and paid well, especially those who work hard at both preaching and teaching. For the Scripture says, "You must not muzzle an ox to keep it from eating as it treads out the grain." And in another place, "Those who work deserve their pay!" (1 Timothy 5:17-18, NLT)

Most of us have given whatever we have given in the past almost exclusively through our local churches. Perhaps in addition to this, we have occasionally sent a few bucks to the Billy Graham Crusade or something like that and maybe put a few dollars in the open Bible on Gideon Sunday at our church. Occasionally we may also have put our pocket change into a plate being passed for the "free-will offering" for representatives of some visiting ministry.

The point is this: we have always thought of our local congregation as the primary beneficiary of our tithes and offerings. Anything given to something outside of our congregation, or outside the denomination it was affiliated with, was considered over and above our regular offering. Our local leaders encouraged us in this manner of giving.

When I was a young Baptist, the song went something like this: were to give our tithe (never any less) to the local church, which in turn gave its "tithe" to the Southern Baptist Convention. Somewhere in between, there was the "association" and the state convention. I don't know exactly how it was all divided up, but this was how the cause of Christ was to be funded. All the larger ministries, such as hospitals, colleges, seminaries, missionary activities, and the like, were funded by the "tithe" that went out from the local congregations. To adapt a term from the Reagan era, we could call this "trickle-up economics." I can presume that something similar happened in other denominations. This model was considered so inviolate by some that they would not even consider putting something into the collection plate of another church that they may be visiting. Anyone who saw value in any other endeavor and wished to contribute to it was taught that such things were considered to be in addition to the tithe given to the local church. The tithe was first to be given to the local congregation before the thought was entertained of giving to anything else.

Now we are out on the road, far away from home. We are being ministered to, and are ministering through, many organizations outside of the local congregation that has been our channel of giving in the past. Just how are we to go about allocating our stewardship of giving now? Is it okay to throw just a few bucks at these other ministries as we have done in the past and give the rest to our local church? Exactly how much do we owe to a hometown church that we only attend perhaps once or twice a year? I believe that these are valid questions for us to ask.

First, let's go back to what we learned in the chapter "What Is 'The Church'?" We saw that the church is the Body of Christ. It is made up of all believers, and Christ is the directing Head. It is safe for us to say, therefore, that anything we contribute to the efforts of believers who are being directed by our Lord, Jesus Christ, is being given to "The Church" in this broader sense.

Local churches and denominations can often be quite provincial in their thinking regarding many matters, including giving, and often they try to teach their members to be so as well. As before, when we took a broader look at what is "The Church," I think that as full-time RV travelers, we need to step back and see the larger picture here as well.

The question of whether all your "purposed" giving should go to your home church or whether it should be split between the various ministries that bless your life is an important consideration. Let me just put forth a thought. As full-time RVers, we take advantage of many ministries that are beyond the local church where we are members. There is a passage of scripture that addresses this:

> The one who is taught the word is to share all good things with
> the one who teaches him. (Galatians 6:6, NASB)

If we partake of a ministry and get benefit from it, we should contribute to it financially.

At this point, before my Baptist friends begin to gather and make plans to run me out of town on the proverbial rail, let me say this: We belong to our home churches. We benefit just by belonging, even though we may not attend very often. If our names are on their roll, they are going forth in their designated community in the name of the Lord Jesus on our behalf. At least a portion of our giving should be directed to our home church. "As a man purposes in his heart, so let him give."

Having said that, I must quickly add also, if we benefit from the ministry of a local church in an area where we are staying, we need to be contributing financially to that church's ministry. A friend of ours attends a local church of her particular denominational preference in the community where she spends the winter. She frequently talks about how wrong she thinks it is that other "snowbirds" attend but do not contribute to this congregation and about how the financial needs are going unmet there because of this neglect. Indeed, it is wrong if we get the benefit from the ministry of a local church, however short a time it may be, and do not make a financial contribution there. Think of how it affects these local churches. In some of the snowbird areas, their attendance in the winter doubles, or even triples, sometimes causing them to have to add an additional worship service to accommodate everyone. What would happen if their offerings remained the same during these times? Talk about a "budget crunch"!

Our park-based churches deserve our support too. Many of these are funded either in part or totally by the parks themselves. Many more are funded by what we put in the offering plates, and that alone. If these are blessing our life out on the road, it is appropriate that we fund them.

Those of you who have a background in the independent, unaffiliated churches, such as the nondenominational, community, or "Bible" churches, are familiar with those congregations' manner of funding missions or other endeavors outside their congregations. Missionaries and other representatives of independent ministries are invited to speak in their churches and thereby solicit pledges either from the congregation as a whole or from individuals within them. This is similar to the way that such organizations as Christian Resort Ministries International and many others are supported. My friends that are in these ministries fund their efforts by what they earn by their outside work and by what they receive from fellow Christians like you and me.

If we get benefit from any other ministry as we are out on the road, we should be open to the idea that God intends us to support that ministry. For example, I am very blessed by the ministry of an independent, nationally syndicated Christian radio station that I can receive in about 90 percent of the locations that I go. Consequently, I feel that God wants me to make a contribution to that ministry. Incidentally, it would be entirely possible for any of the larger denominational groups to underwrite their own national radio ministry of this nature, funded by that which they collect from their member churches. So far, however, none of them have seen fit to engage in such an endeavor. This, of course, does not keep some denominational leaders from criticizing their members who choose to contribute to these nondenominational parachurch ministries instead of giving the same amount to their denomination.

There is a fact that we have to face: the local churches and their denominations are not reaching out to full-time RVers. It doesn't matter in the end whether they are just unaware of us or whether they think that what we are doing is improper or they just don't care; the effect is still the same. As I said before, they almost always welcome us in their churches *when we seek them out*, but when it comes to them reaching out to us, they won't touch us with the proverbial ten-foot pole. In some rare cases, such as we will mention in the next chapter, they provide us with opportunities to be involved in ministries that they sponsor. There are, however, only isolated cases that I have seen that local churches, or the denominations that they represent, are seeking to minister to the occupants of RV parks. The reason that so many of us get involved in parachurch organizations, such as Christian Resort Ministries, is that they are involved with us in ways that most local churches are not.

There are many ministries that are worthy of our contributions. As we travel about the nation, we have opportunity to see some of these in action and to contribute to them. While money is often "tight" for many of us on fixed incomes, I have had opportunity to meet many full-timers who are blessed financially and are in a position to be very generous with their money. In either case, we have the opportunity to be partners with God and with those who are called to these ministries that bless our lives and the lives of many others. We can all afford to be generous in our support of them.

A word of caution is in order before we proceed. We need to be careful about contributing to anyone who simply hangs up a cross and asks for a contribution. A large dose of discernment is called for here. Those that we support financially should first of all be true believers and, second, they should show the obvious anointing of the Holy Spirit on their ministry, obvious by the blessing they impart to us and to others. As Paul instructed the Thessalonian Christians,

> Test everything. Hold on to the good. Avoid every kind of evil.
> (1 Thessalonians 5:20-21, NIV)

Giving to the Poor

There is much said in the New Testament about giving to the poor. Much that Jesus taught deals with having compassion for them. Paul's statements about giving, many of which we have reviewed in this chapter, were offered in the context of the collections that were being taken up for the poor in Jerusalem by the other churches. Again, I don't know why Jerusalem seemed to have such a problem when none of the other churches seemed to be so impoverished, but it seems that the funds were always flowing from the other churches to Jerusalem.

Jesus reminded us that "you will always have the poor among you" (John 12:8, NIV). I have never taken this to be a commandment, but it is certainly a statement of fact.

In Jesus' day, there was not the welfare system that we have in our world today. If you were poor in that era, you were pretty much on your own and dependent on the generosity of family, friends, or strangers. In our own modern, secular humanist society, we have come to believe that the care of the poor should be delegated to the government. It is interesting to note that this belief that the poor should be cared for by all of society is largely an outgrowth of Christian teaching.

It is far beyond the scope of this book to comment as to whether the care of the poor in our society is being carried out effectively. We acknowledge, however, a welfare system which is in place, in America at least, that makes it unnecessary for anyone to go without their basic needs of food and shelter. One thing needs to be noted, however. The secular humanist domination of caring for the poor through government has made it increasingly difficult, if not impossible, for us as Christians to bring to the poor the one thing that we can give that the government cannot give, that is, the Gospel message that only we can tell. It is *the* message that will truly change their lives. Jesus asked,

> "What do you benefit if you gain the whole world but lose your own soul? Is anything worth more than your soul?" (Mark 8:36-37, NLT).

Indeed, what does it profit if we feed the poor, house the homeless, and alleviate suffering on every level and none of the recipients of these ministerings know that the reason that we do it is because of our commitment to our Savior, who wants to be their Savior too?

There are many levels at which we Christians can engage in ministry to the poor of our society. The presence of an elaborate and comprehensive welfare system in our society does not absolve us from this ministry. Moreover, we need to be zealous to assure that the "Good News is preached to the poor" (Luke 4:18).

And then, there is the poor of the remainder of the world. The impoverished in our own nation look wealthy in comparison to many of the average citizens of many underdeveloped nations. Once again, we need to be careful not to give our money to anyone who asks, but to determine that the organization is worthy of our support and that the support is actually getting through to the people we are trying to reach.

Many of the denominations and the nondenominational mission societies are reaching out to both the physically and the spiritually poor of the world and deserve our support. In any case, we should follow Paul's example:

> Their only suggestion [for my ministry] was that we keep on helping the poor, which I have always been eager to do. (Galatians 2:10, NLT)

Stingy versus Generous

Another fact that we must face here is that we "seniors" as a group have acquired a reputation for being a stingy bunch. While I am not sure that this is a deserved reputation in all cases, I have observed that many of us, myself included, are very "tight" with our money. Many times, the cares and worries of our everyday lives and the financial concerns for our own families have made us quite careful about how we distribute our money.

We talked earlier in this chapter about how the Spirit of the Lord transformed the believers in the early church from an attitude of self-centeredness and stinginess to an attitude of generosity toward one another and toward the cause of Christ and the furtherance of the Gospel.

Applying all due caution to see that our money is being given to the right parties and being directed to the right places, it certainly behooves us to loosen up and be generous as we seek to become partners with Christ in the support of His work in the world and of the ministries that bless our lives.

God Does Not Need Our Money

We are often under the mistaken impression that God could not get by without our support. We mistake the begging attitude of some of His misguided servants with the idea that He needs our money to get by. God doesn't need our money. The idea we have expressed in this chapter and the last that everything comes from Him is not an abstract concept. It is a fact. He said through the Psalmist,

> I do not need the bulls from your barns
> or the goats from your pens.
> For all the animals of the forest are mine,
> and I own the cattle on a thousand hills.
> I know every bird on the mountains,
> and all the animals of the field are mine.
> If I were hungry, I would not tell you,
> for all the world is mine and everything in it. (Psalm 50:9-12, NLT)

If we believe in Him at all, and if we take His word seriously in any measure, we will agree that we are but managers and our stewardship of our money is a trust He has given to us to manage until He returns, or until we return to Him. Taking this responsibility seriously will bring two specific results:

We will honor God in the way we use *all* of our wealth.

We will find ways to appropriately fund God's work with our wealth.

> Every man according as he purposeth in his heart, so let him give.
> (2 Corinthians 9:7, KJV)

CHAPTER 12

Stewardship: Part C, Ministry

Therefore, if anyone is in Christ, he is a new creation; the old has gone, the new has come! All this is from God, who reconciled us to himself through Christ and gave us the ministry of reconciliation: that God was reconciling the world to himself in Christ, not counting men's sins against them. And he has committed to us the message of reconciliation.

—2 Corinthians 5:17-19 (NIV)

I WISH I had a five-dollar bill for every time I have read a sign in front of a church that said something to the order "Pastor, Rev. Bill Smith; Ministers, everyone."

The idea of every Christian being a "minister" has become a cliché, at least among Evangelicals, yet not everyone takes this concept to heart. Like many of the things that we do in church, what we say is often different than what we do. And for the many of us that are serious about this matter, we are often uncertain what this means in our particular lives, and we expend a lot of energy and prayer trying to determine what our "ministry" is and what God wants us to do.

Our ministry to the world, as suggested by the title of this chapter, is yet another aspect of our whole-life stewardship. If indeed our personalities and our opportunities and all we have in this life come from God, our ministry to the world is no more, or no less, than an extension of our continued management of what He has given and continues to give us.

In chapter 2, we spoke of spiritual gifts given to each believer for the building up of the Body of Christ. Ministry is the context in which we will exercise these spiritual gifts and in which that "building up" will occur.

We owe it to our Lord, as good managers, to develop our gifts, talents, opportunities, and such and use them for His Glory and the furtherance of His objectives in this world.

We do not need a "proof text" to bring forth the idea that is implied throughout the Bible, that there is something that each of us is uniquely qualified to do—something that the unique path of our life has brought us to that no one else can accomplish in quite the same way as can we. We want it said of us as of Esther, "Who knows but that you have come . . . for such [an opportunity] as this?" (Esther 4:14, NIV).

That book of Esther is an interesting story in itself and one that bears reading in regard to what we are discussing at this point in this book. Oddly, the book of Esther is the only book in the Bible that does not mention God by name or by inference. For this reason, there have been some in times past that have suggested that perhaps this book does not really belong in the Bible, and many have been reluctant to teach or preach from it. Yet all one has to do is to read that story and reflect a bit upon what is happening in it, and we can readily see the hand of God at work as He moves in the events of this story. We need not go into extensive commentary here. The book of Esther is a story about two Jewish cousins, Esther and Mordecai, being placed strategically by God in the kingdom of Persia. They take advantage of the somewhat difficult opportunities that are presented to them, even at the peril of their own lives (Esther 4:16); and in the end, they save God's people from annihilation and keep the road clear for the coming of God's plan for redemption through Jesus Christ. I urge you to read this marvelous story sometime soon.

Because of the absence of any reference to God, it is difficult to determine if Esther and Mordecai were aware of their divinely ordered destiny. Perhaps many of us will not be aware of such a thing in our own lives. But they met with their divine appointment and did what they knew to be the right thing. The rest, as they say, is history.

If there is a "proof text" for the idea that God forms all of us and places us into the opportunities of our lives, these words from God to Jeremiah seem to fill the bill.

"Before I formed you in the womb I knew you, before you were born I set you apart; I appointed you as a prophet to the nations."
(Jeremiah 1:5, NIV)

Unless we talk ourselves into believing that Jeremiah was the only man in history who was known before the womb by Almighty God and the only one who was set apart by Him for a purpose, we have to see a level of application of this truth for each and every one of us as well.

Every believer in Jesus Christ has a ministry. Even as Jeremiah was "appointed . . . as a prophet to the nations," so each one of us is "appointed" to do something for God that is uniquely ours to do. It will perhaps not be as spectacular as being a prophet to the nations in the manner of someone like Jeremiah or Billy Graham. We may not even be fully aware of what it is that we are appointed to do. But if we follow the Holy Spirit, we will find our God-given destiny.

On the morning of the day I began to write this chapter in earnest, my daily Bible reading was Acts 9, the conversion of Saul. I am sure we are all familiar with the story. The part that reached out and grabbed me was where Christ spoke to the reluctant Ananaias:

> But the Lord said, "Go and do what I say. For Saul is my chosen instrument to take my message to the Gentiles and to kings, as well as to the people of Israel." (Acts 9:15, NLT)

Saul (of course, later to be known as the apostle Paul) is called by God "my chosen instrument"! It didn't matter that he had just been hunting down Christians and dragging them off to imprisonment and death. It didn't matter that at that time Saul had already made up his mind that "the Way" (Acts 9:2) was not only a falsehood but a serious threat to the Jewish faith. Christ confronted Saul on that road to Damascus, and Saul recognized Him as Lord, and from that moment on, Saul followed Him and Him alone. Saul became His "chosen instrument."

Christ is an equal-opportunity employer. He has chosen us even as much as He did Saul, and the idea that He hasn't chosen each believer for something is indefensible, either biblically of logically.

Labels and Pigeonholes

Having said that, I think that it is important not to confuse ministries with labels. In our attempts to understand and give order to our world, we like to place labels on things. We are a "writer" or a "singer" or a "carpenter" or any other number of labels we can adopt to organize our lives and help us to understand ourselves and our place here in this world. In another chapter, we talked about our human tendency to put restrictions and narrow definitions upon categories that we invent ourselves. These are sometimes referred to as "pigeonholes," so named after the little partitioned nest boxes used by those who raise pigeons. Let us remember at this point that God transcends our labels and categories. Let us not allow ourselves or Him to be confined by them.

Sometimes we want God to give us a neat packaged idea of what our ministry to the world will be. We presume also that it will be the same throughout our lifetime. If I have not learned anything else in the last sixty-plus years, I have learned that God, who is unchanging, changes our plans and the direction of our lives regularly. How many of you, fifty years ago, would have thought that you would be out on the road full-time today?

There is an old Jewish proverb (not found in the Bible) that I have heard quoted on many occasions in recent years. It goes something like this: "If you want to make God laugh, tell Him your plans." I didn't like this proverb when I first heard it. I had always thought of it as an excessively cynical remark that depicted a somewhat sadistic God who enjoyed disappointing us and ruining our ideas about how our lives should go. I have now come to see it in a different way. If God is moved to laughter over our plans, it is because He sees the big picture and already knows what is going to happen. It is sort of like when one of my daughters used to tell me about her plans to become a rock star. She is now an attorney and, to my recollection, has never sung on a stage in her life.

My own story, as I reflect back, is certainly an example of what I am talking about. When I was a senior in high school, I felt very distinctly that the Lord was leading me to pursue a career in "the ministry." I began to pursue my education as one would expect, first college, then seminary. At first, I was in demand as a preacher for filling pulpits and for special meetings. Then I got an opportunity to start a church and to be its pastor. This is when it all started to turn around. I began to sense that He was leading in a different direction. To make the long story short, by the time I was about halfway through seminary, I felt very strongly led to drop out and pursue a career in law enforcement. It would be easy and in accordance with "conventional wisdom," to say at this point, that I may have originally been mistaken about God's intentions for me, and I felt for many years that this was the case. As I look back and especially since I began to write this book, I can see that the theological education and the experience of leading churches, as well as the "education" I got from twenty-five years as a police officer and supervisor, followed by a decade of living full-time on the road, was exactly what I needed to bring me to this point.

I think that I have wanted to write a book since I was about eight or nine years old. As I have reflected on this desire in my adulthood, I have always felt that indeed I would like to write a book, but it always seemed that I really had nothing to say that someone else hadn't already said much better that I could have. Then one day, during the time that our Adventureland Bible study group was studying *The Purpose Driven Life*, I felt the Spirit of the Lord say to me that, yes, I did have something to say. Over the preceding decade, He had led me out of my "wandering period" and had restored me to following His path and leadership. He had set me out on the road and was continuing to teach me how to follow and stay close to Him in this RV lifestyle. I finally had found the book-writing opportunity for which I had searched for so long.

So now, here I am, an old retired guy who never wanted to work after retirement. I have two seasonal jobs and travel around in a motor home. I thought my days of Bible teaching were over, but it seems that they have started again, with no apparent end in sight, and that's just fine with me. I see my present ministry as writing my blog, leading my small-group Bible study, and, of course, writing this book. I feel very strongly led to write and am continually encouraged by my Christian friends to do this. Is my ministry to be a writer? I guess that time will tell. I talked to God this morning about my next book. I think I heard Him chuckle a little.

So what are your plans? How do you see your area of ministry? Is it the same as it was twenty years ago? What do you see for the days ahead? I once heard someone describe life as a building with several rooms connected by a hallway. We begin to walk down the hallway with a certain destination in mind, but on the way, we pass a room in which we see an interesting activity that we feel compelled to join, and in we go. We who belong to Jesus Christ are on a great adventure of following the Holy Spirit down that hallway. He is our guide. He will prepare us as we go today for what lies ahead tomorrow. He will "teach us all things, and guide us into all truth" (John 14:16, 16:13) concerning how each of us can uniquely minister to the world. The apostle John also later summarized:

> But you have received the Holy Spirit, and he lives within you, so you don't need anyone to teach you what is true. For the Spirit teaches you all things, and what he teaches is true—it is not a lie. So continue in what he has taught you, and continue to live in Christ. (1 John 2:27, NLT)

Reconciliation, the "Big Umbrella"

Our text verse at the beginning of the chapter told us that "God was reconciling the world to himself in Christ" and further that "He has committed to us the message of reconciliation." At the center, therefore, of all of our efforts at ministry will be the act of helping people find reconciliation with their Creator.

In English, the word "reconcile" means "to cause to be friendly or harmonious again."[31] The Greek word that is translated as "reconcile" in the Bible is used specifically by the New Testament writers to describe the restoration of one's relationship with God.[32] Whatever ministry we perform, it will have as its either direct or indirect objective to make people right with God through Jesus Christ. We who are already reconciled to God through Christ are the only ones who can carry that message to the world.

The Two Phases of Reconciliation

There are two phases to the ministry of reconciliation. The first involves bringing people into this right relationship with God for the very first time. We sometimes call this "saving the lost." We don't hear the term "getting saved" very much anymore. Probably because of the negative connotation that has come out of the various presentations of the media, such as the mid-twentieth-century novel *Elmer Gantry* or, more recently, the twenty-first-century movie *Saved*. These represent a literary genre that seeks to discredit those who try to win the lost. And let's face it, the scandals of the last half century involving televangelists and other Evangelical Christian ministers have not helped the cause either.

In chapter 1, I chose to call my own salvation experience a "redemptive encounter," and if you want to use that term, feel free. The point I am trying to make is that there is such a thing as bringing people into a relationship with God through Jesus Christ for the first time. We frequently call this "evangelism." Evangelism means to tell the Good News of salvation in Christ, and it is implied that we give folks the opportunity to respond and also perhaps help them, by the power of the Holy Spirit, to make that response.

Evangelism is a big task. It involves Christians who have the specific gift of evangelism in the front line of the advance. We often forget, though, that evangelism is a whole church effort and there are many who work behind the front lines, planting the seeds and doing the deeds that prepare the hearts to receive the Gospel. The church janitor who makes the sanctuary a clean and pleasant place to be is as important a part of the work of evangelism as the pastor who gives the invitation. In my own experience, I can identify several people who were responsible for my decision to answer Christ's call to me. In the end, it is the Holy Spirit who does the whole work of evangelism. Saving people is God's business, and we must see that we are but participants in this phase of the ministry of reconciliation.

The second phase of the ministry of reconciliation is then to bring those who are now initially reconciled closer and closer to Him. We have, to this point, called this by the biblical terminology "building up the Body of Christ" (Ephesians 4:12).

Once again, we need not see ourselves as being involved with either one phase or the other, for both are the whole task of the whole church. It is essential that we recognize this phase as a legitimate part of the ministry of reconciliation. People need not only to come to Christ but to draw ever closer to Him throughout their lives. Many of the problems that we experience within the church today are a direct result of believers' failure to grow and become closer to our Lord.

In addition, there are many who have wandered away, even as I did, and are in need of someone to bring the influence of the Holy Spirit back into their lives. I myself feel a burden to participate in things that will "save the saved"[33] and help others to find again the joy of the Lord in their lives that they once had.

So How Do I Know What to Do?

In the earlier chapter about whole-life stewardship, we talked about how that our wealth, our personalities, and our opportunities are things that are given to us by God. Even the fact that you are in this country rather than another is a work of God in your life. I would go to China or Turkmenistan or wherever God wanted me, but considering all the learning of language, culture, and such that I would have to do in places like that, I don't consider this to be likely. After all, I am running out of time. The point is, we are where we are, we know what we know, and we have experienced what we have experienced because of what the Lord has been able to do with us up to this time. What God wants us to do with our future will most likely have its beginning in the present. There will most likely be an obvious first step that we can take right where we are. With His guidance, we can take advantage of the opportunities that are before us.

A valid question, then, in light of all God has given us is, "What do I want to do?" Somehow we have gotten the idea that God's will is necessarily at odds with our own will (which in fact it sometimes is) and that it will be something that we find totally unpleasant and distasteful to do. I once visited the Web site of a church that I was considering attending. There were three pastors on staff, and in their profiles on that Web site, each told about having "surrendered to preach" at some point in their lives. Now I know that this is just terminology, but there are many terms that they could have used instead. Having heard one of them use this expression didn't faze me too much, but when all three used it and did so in a context that made it sound like it was the last thing that they wanted to do, I couldn't help but think that if these guys have that hard of a time following the Spirit's leadership, I certainly can't expect them to be able to help me follow the Lord in my life!

Let us remember that we are reconciled to God through Jesus Christ. Let us remember that we have the Holy Spirit within us and alongside us. As we saw earlier, Jesus said, "My sheep [know] my voice," and that learning to listen to the voice of Jesus is a necessary part of our Christian growth. The change of heart that we all experience when we come to Christ may not immediately result in changed habits, but the one thing that does change is that we *want* to please him. If we *desire* to do something in our regenerated heart, chances are it is what God wants, at least for now. Our passions are a part of that of which God has made us stewards. Who wants to do something that they cannot be passionate about? And who wants to deal with anyone who cannot be enthusiastic about what they are doing?

Having said that, we also need to take into consideration that we are all a work in progress, and we should all take some time in prayer to analyze our desires. He will make it known to us, if we are willing to listen, whether our desire is from Him or from our self. If you are having trouble recognizing Christ's voice, perhaps ministry to the world is not something you should be concerned about right now. Learn to listen; then learn to minister.

Another valid question we can ask ourselves is, "What am I good at?" The really good thing I have noticed about the community of full-time RVers is that there are so many people among us that "used to be somebody" and consequently there is a very excellent talent pool here.

And let us also ask, "What can I learn to be good at?" Contrary to the old saying, you can, in fact, teach an old dog new tricks. Many of us have learned new skills in our old age, and certainly our Lord can take us from where we are, in terms of our skills, to new and exciting places that we never dreamed of before.

All ministry will build up the church and will advance the cause of Christ and the Gospel if it has as its overall objective to reconcile people to God through Jesus Christ. Let me introduce two categories, then, which will help us to clarify our subject. Basically, ministries will take place in one of two settings: in church (that is, a local congregation or denomination) and outside of church. Each of us may have a ministry to perform in either or both settings. As we have previously warned, let us not presume it will be either one or the other.

Church Ministries

There are many things that we are called upon to do that will be a function within the meetings or the extended ministry of our local congregations. There will be some who are reading this whom God has called or will call to be prophets, evangelists, pastors, or teachers (Ephesians 4:11). These are certainly what make the church function, and while most of us will indeed be laymen, Christ needs these essential parts of His Body for it to function as it is intended. A friend of mine, who is very biblically knowledgeable and has a passionate heart for the Lord, found himself one day to have an opportunity to be a pastor in his RV park, even though he had never been a pastor before. Be open to the idea that the Lord may use you in ways that He has never used you before and that are out of the ordinary for you. Remember, it is we who define what is ordinary. The Spirit of God does not always recognize our boundaries.

In addition, there are many other functions that are necessary to keep congregations running as they should. Many are talented in the area of music. My observation has been that music programs throughout Christ's church, and particularly in park churches, are in need of talented (or even semi talented) musicians to keep them going. How sad indeed it would be if there were no music or when there is "bad" music in church.

I have a very deep appreciation for those who are willing to host the small-group Bible studies in their homes. It is often easier to find small-group leaders than hosts. A leader can lead in many locations on different days, but only one can be a host at a time, generally. Those who host well are "worthy of double honor" in my opinion.

Many of the ministries that take place behind the scenes are also extremely necessary. The ushers, the maintenance persons, the business managers, all perform a vital role without which the local congregations and park churches could not function.

Another vital ministry that is sometimes not even recognized as a ministry is to just show up. Without anyone there to participate, the leaders could get pretty lonely. Seriously, there is a function that is performed by being present and being a good example of what a participant should be. By showing up and participating, we say a lot to the world about who we are and what Christ means to us.

A former pastor of mine once told a story about a man who was completely deaf. In spite of this handicap, the man came to church every Sunday and sat in one of the front seats. This was before our present day, when deaf-signing interpreters were readily available. One day, someone asked this man why he continued to go to church when he couldn't hear a thing. The brother replied, "I just want everyone to know whose side I'm on!" Likewise, sometimes we need to show the world whose side we are on. The support that we show not only for our leaders but for what the Lord is doing in our community of faith means so much. Paul reminds us,

> Our bodies have many parts, and God has put each part just where he wants it. How strange a body would be if it had only one part! Yes, there are many parts, but only one body. The eye can never say to the hand, "I don't need you." The head can't say to the feet, "I don't need you."
>
> In fact, some parts of the body that seem weakest and least important are actually the most necessary. (1 Corinthians 12:18-22, NLT)

As we have pointed out already, local churches are not reaching into the RV community, so it is essential that believers who are RVers reach out and "be the church" within our own community. Perhaps that is why God has placed so many of us out here.

It is also important that RV Christians "reach out" to the local churches and bring an understanding to them of who we are. Perhaps if they get to know us, one day they too will partner with us in ministering to our community.

Into the World

I think it is clear that it was part of Jesus' plan for His church that they would interface with the world on a daily basis, even as He and His disciples did. Even in His prayer for all believers He prayed,

I'm not asking you to take them out of the world, but to keep them safe from the evil one. (John 17:15, NLT)

I have quoted the passage in Ephesians 4 so often in this book that we probably know it by heart by now. God gave what I have called the "pastoral gifts," those used in the meetings of the church for the purpose of equipping believers when they go from the church into the world "for the work of the ministry." How often have you heard the pastor or the worship leader end a worship service with the admonition "Go forth and serve the Lord" or something like that? I have yet to hear one of them say, "Come back next week and serve the Lord."

Unfortunately, many of us continue to believe that ministry is something that takes place only in church. I had opportunity to spend time in fellowship with one of my old friends the other day. It was clear that it was his deep-seated belief that how good a Christian you were had a direct relationship to what you did inside the local church.

I think that I can say that it is generally accepted that this was not how it was done in the New Testament Church. While there are not all that many specifics about how they went about it, the first-century church simply could not have gone forth into all the world as they did if they had been solely dependent on "professional" clergy. The "laity" must certainly have played a central role in spreading the Gospel at the opportunity and leadership of the Holy Spirit when they went out into the world in their daily lives.

In fact, that whole concept of the dichotomy of clergy and laity, though it had some beginnings in the second century, is largely a product of the Middle Ages rather than the New Testament. If the Lord leaves me here or delays His coming long enough, I would like this to be the subject of a future book. Suffice it to say here that the medieval ideas of sacred and secular, clergy and laity still permeate our thinking now into the twenty-first century. This is a dangerous idea that we need to beware of and to avoid.

There are many ways that we can serve our Lord and minister in His name to the world as we go about our daily lives. The following is not an exhaustive list but a few suggested areas:

On the Job

There are many of us who are still working in some form or another. We are either "Workampers" or operating home businesses or volunteering or something like that. Paul tells us, as he told the Colossians,

> Whatever you do, work at it with all your heart, as working for the Lord, not for men, since you know that you will receive an inheritance from the Lord as a reward. It is the Lord Christ you are serving. (Colossians 3:23-24, NIV)

I have observed a marvelous thing at my workplace at Adventureland. The quality of the experience that our guests have has greatly increased over the eleven seasons that I have worked there and particularly since the Adventureland Congregation has been in existence. This is not simply due to the fact that seniors make better workers. It is, in my opinion, because fully one-fourth of the employees there are committed Christians and that so many of them take the foregoing scripture to heart. The Christian Workampers, as well as the local believers, have made all the difference in this situation.

Often, when we have visiting ministers leading our employee worship service, they and their families are given the opportunity to spend the day "playing" in the park afterwards. I frequently tell them when I see them during the day, "Now it's our turn to minister to you." I have had many tell me that they truly felt ministered to while visiting with us. Perhaps some realize for the first time that we who belong to the Lord are truly performing a ministry to the world in that setting.

Many Christians of my acquaintance see their work as a means to an end, to enable them to pay their bills and support their church. They have not come to see their occupations as an avenue to ministry. When we work as though Jesus Christ is our boss, it makes a difference in the lives of our clientele and our coworkers, as well as enhancing the credibility of the Christian message in the world at large.

Family

Many of us now have more free time than we had before. We are using our RV lifestyle to take greater advantage of opportunities to spend time with our families. Often, this gives us a chance to minister to our loved ones. This can take as many forms as there are families, but I think that we can all readily see ways that we can minister to our families. Being a Christian parent or grandparent or brother or sister or whatever relationship and being involved in the lives of family members in the name of Christ is as much of an important ministry as anything else we can do.

Parachurch Activities

Activities in which Christians perform ministries that are not directly sponsored by particular denominations or local churches are called "parachurch" activities. In these ministries, Christians of many congregations and across denominational lines are involved. These are such things as the Gideons, Navigators, and other similar interdenominational ministries.

In my own mind, there is some question as to whether these should even be called "parachurch activities." Going back to chapter 3, all believers *are* the church. These activities, generally speaking, are the efforts of Christian believers who see a need that should be filled and have joined forces with other Christians whose hearts are likewise burdened about that same need, without regard to congregational or denominational affiliation.

I think that it is important that these so-called parachurch activities do not supplant the work of the local church. They are not in competition with local churches, nor are they to function as substitutes for the local church. They are not ministries unto themselves but a part of the "ministry of reconciliation" of "*The* Church" at large. Charles Colson and Ellen Vaughn, in *Being the Body*, make the following statement, with which I agree wholeheartedly:

> Whether these parachurch ministries are building up the Body is perhaps the best test of their biblical fidelity. Those that aren't cooperating with and equipping the work of local churches run the risk of ending up promoting their own cause over the good of the Body and thus being outside God's plan. (This has been a real problem among evangelicals. One great strength of the movement is its vitality: independent, dynamic leaders raising up powerful organizations to do important work. But human nature being what it is, this can also be a weakness when those same leaders become protective of their turf or fall into the trap of the personality cult.)[34]

There is another side to this coin, however. It seems to me that the same thing could be said about many of those in leadership positions in the local churches. These congregational leaders are not any less susceptible to turf wars or personality cults and can just as easily supplant the important work that is being done by the parachurch ministries. I have seen this sort of thing happen in my work with the Gideon ministry. As we have already noted, many ministries that, in my view, are performing an essential service are operating apart from the local congregations and denominations. The local churches and their denominations apparently feel no need or calling to perform these ministries. Perhaps this is the way that our Lord has designed for this to happen, but neither the churches nor the parachurch ministries should have to feel threatened by each other as long as the Lord's work is getting done (see Mark 9:38-41).

My observation has been that those who are under the influence of the Holy Spirit tend to be respectful to others in ministries outside their circle of experience. As we have mentioned in past discussions, when the Spirit of God is not allowed to be involved in the work of a Christian organization (be it local church, denominational, or parachurch), the egos of men usually rise to fill the gap. Perhaps another "test of biblical fidelity" in addition to the one mentioned in the quote above might be whether the leadership of either the church or the parachurch group feels threatened by the existence of the other.

"Mission Projects"

There are also many opportunities for RVers to minister through local church, parachurch and denominational organizations by getting involved in what are commonly called "Mission Projects." The Escapee's Christian Fellowship BOF has several of them listed on their Web site. There are also others, such as Nomads (United Methodist), Laborers for Christ (Lutheran), and such cross-denominational organizations as SOWERS (Servants on Wheels Ever Ready) and MMAP (Mobile Missionary Assistance Program), just to name a few.

Most of these involve the RVers doing "grunt work," like building or repairing facilities, doing office work, and all sorts of things of this nature that would be too expensive for the groups involved to hire done. This is not a bad thing. In fact, it reminds me of those first servants in Acts who took on the task of food distribution so that the apostles could devote themselves to "prayer and the ministry of the word" (Acts 6:1-7).

Please don't misunderstand. I do not mean the term "grunt work" in any derogatory or demeaning way. Some of my friends who have done this type of thing are really blessed by the experience, and I am sure the recipients of their efforts were blessed as well. It is my fond hope, however, that one day these organizations will recognize another aspect of the abilities of full-time RVers and will utilize their talents in such areas as teaching Bible studies, music ministry, and even speaking in pulpits and giving special presentations in worship services and other church meetings. I believe that it would be greatly beneficial to everyone involved if these "mission projects" gave the full-timers the opportunity to exercise both their physical talents and their spiritual gifts.

There is a couple that we read about in the Bible who, I believe, are a perfect example of what we are trying to say about every Christian having a ministry. This would be Paul's friends and fellow tentmakers Priscilla and Aquila.

When we first meet them in the New Testament, they, being Jews, had been expelled from Rome (Acts 18). It appears that they were already believers when they met Paul in Corinth, and some speculate that they may have been among the three thousand who responded at Pentecost. It is recorded that Paul met them and joined them in the tentmaking trade while he was in Corinth. They went with Paul to Ephesus after that and stayed there while he went on to Antioch. They are well-known for having taken aside the great speaker Apollos, who had been a disciple of John the Baptist, and witnessing to him regarding the resurrected and living Christ.

Priscilla and Aquila opened their home and hosted meetings of the church in many of the locations where we read about them. (Remember what I said about small-group hosts?) Their home was where a group of the Ephesian church met (1 Corinthians 16:19). We later find them back in Rome once again with their home being used as a meeting place for the church (Romans 16:3-5).

Later still, we find them back in Ephesus (2 Timothy 4:19). It is definite that they moved around a lot (kind of like we do). We are not told whether they moved about from place to place from some economic or social necessity or whether they did it intentionally to be a part of the furtherance of the Gospel. Tentmaking was their trade, and tents are temporary dwellings. They may have had opportunity to relocate often as temporary dwellings were needed in various places in the Roman Empire. Some have speculated that they followed groups of the Roman army and made or repaired tents for them as needed. It is just as easy to believe that they moved about at the opportunity of the Holy Spirit. I have a picture of them in my mind moving from place to place, packing all their belongings and tentmaking supplies into some kind of horse-drawn cart (a first-century RV if you will). It is crystal clear, however, that wherever they were, they were servants of Christ in the communities in which they settled.

They appeared not to be exercising any of the "pastoral" spiritual gifts usually associated with what we now term the clergy as we discussed earlier. Since they were so able to teach Apollos, it may have been that they taught or led the groups that met in their home. It would seem from the contexts in which they are usually mentioned that they did not consider themselves in the same category as the apostles and elders and such, but they were solid members of whatever local church that they were affiliated with and could be depended upon to support and "build up the Body of Christ" in whatever way the Holy Spirit led them.

It has been my pleasure over the last few years to know many modern-day Priscillas and Aquilas. They are RVers that serve their Lord as they travel. You usually know them when you meet them. While perhaps they are not always "in your face" about your spiritual life, there is just something about them that gives you the idea that they are in touch with the Holy Spirit. As you get to know them, their conversation and their habits, a picture begins to emerge of one who belongs to Jesus Christ.

There are in fact so many of these folks of my acquaintance that they are too numerous for me to mention them all. They represent as many stories of the grace of God as there are of them. These are they who are "going forth in the Name." These are they who are changing their world and making a difference in the RV community. This is Ministry that we all take our part in the Body of Christ and that the church goes forth in His name.

CHAPTER 13

The "Fishbowl" Lifestyle

Dear friends, I warn you as "temporary residents and foreigners" to keep away from worldly desires that wage war against your very souls. Be careful to live properly among your unbelieving neighbors. Then even if they accuse you of doing wrong, they will see your honorable behavior, and they will give honor to God when he judges the world.

—1 Peter 2:12 (NLT)

WHEN I WAS a policeman, we used to say that we lived in a "fishbowl," that is, our lives were very visible (wearing recognizable uniforms and driving distinctly marked vehicles), and scarcely anything we did was hidden from view. This extended even into our private lives, as everyone knew who we were. A person could go for years and not know what some of their neighbors did for a living, but everyone knew which neighbor was the policeman. We also had a sense of not only being constantly scrutinized but also being held to a higher standard than was the rest of the world.

This same thing is also true for the Christian. As soon as anyone learns that you are a believer in Jesus Christ, all eyes are upon you. They want to see if we live up to an artificial standard of righteousness that they have superimposed upon us, which, of course, we do not, for no one can. They are waiting like vultures to see us fall. We are being watched!

How often have we heard an unbeliever speak ill of a brother or sister in Christ because of their shortcomings? According to our text above, Peter saw this coming. He probably experienced it himself. And so he warns us to be sure to live properly among our unbelieving neighbors. They are not only judging us, but the very validity of the Gospel message we are bringing to them by what they see. Of course, we know that it was because of our failure at righteousness that Christ gave us His, but they don't really understand this: "The natural man does not receive the things of the Spirit of God" (1 Corinthians 2:14).

And certainly the Christian full-time RVer will be subject to this "fishbowl" existence more so than most of our brothers and sisters in Christ. We will live in small (RV) houses that are close together. Sometimes we are so close to our neighbors that we can literally reach out our windows and touch the rig next door! It is hard to have a conversation in the privacy of our own homes without the folks in the rig next door being able to hear. We often spend a lot of time outside where all can have a better view. We live in communities that are much akin to small towns and where we will be interacting with our neighbors with a closeness that few others experience in regular communities. This is at once a problem and an opportunity.

Separateness in the Old and New Testaments

Most of us like to hang out with people with whom we have something in common. The more others are like ourselves, the more we like to be with them. This is a natural reaction.

As Christians, we often like to hang out with other Christians. We enjoy Christian fellowship, and if nothing else, we know we can talk about our relationship with God and not be ridiculed. Also, in the nurturing relationships within the Body of Christ, we find the spiritual nourishment in which a large part of our Christian growth takes place. It is very easy for us to get into one of those "comfort zones" that we have mentioned frequently and to take the idea of being "separate" to a place that Jesus never intended it to go.

This kind of "separateness" is also appealing to us because it removes us from a certain amount of temptation to which we are exposed when we are in the world at large. If we just hang out with our church group, there are many life issues we simply don't have to face. If we look at the world with our "separated face," they too will avoid us. Sometimes we are saying unconsciously to them, "Leave me alone, or I'll hit you with my Bible!" we have a tendency to favor a kind of separateness like that which we see God's people practicing in the Old Testament.

The concept of "separateness" has some fundamental differences in the way it is seen in the Old and New Testaments.

In the Old Testament, for instance, the nation of Israel was, to a large degree, physically separated from its neighbor nations. They had obvious trade and commercial relationships with the other nations, but they did not live intermingled with them as Christians do among nonbelievers. A Jew living outside Israel before the Babylonian captivity was as rare as a Gentile living within Israel. While some insignificant intermingling was present, God was frequently admonishing His Hebrew people to stay away from the other nations and particularly warning them not to intermarry with the Gentiles. The reason for this is clear: the other nations more frequently had a bad influence on the Jews than the Jews had a good influence on them.

All of this was about to change. The prophet Jeremiah announced the future coming of the New Covenant with these words:

> "The day is coming," says the Lord, "when I will make a new covenant with the people of Israel and Judah. This covenant will not be like the one I made with their ancestors when I took them by the hand and brought them out of the land of Egypt. They broke that covenant, though I loved them as a husband loves his wife," says the Lord.

> "But this is the new covenant I will make with the people of Israel on that day," says the Lord. "I will put my instructions deep within them, and I will write them on their hearts. I will be their God, and they will be my people. And they will not need to teach their neighbors, nor will they need to teach their relatives, saying, 'You should know the Lord.' For everyone, from the least to the greatest, will know me already," says the Lord. "And I will forgive their wickedness, and I will never again remember their sins." (Jeremiah 31:31-34, NLT; also compare Hebrews 10)

Under the New Covenant, we have the Holy Spirit within us, and now it is possible for us to be out among the unbelievers and still be the people that Christ wants us to be and to be His witnesses to that unbelieving world rather than being led astray by it.

The nation of Israel was not charged with the task of making Jews out of all the nations of the world. There were occasional Gentiles who came to see that Jehovah God was the one true God, and they followed Him, adopting the ways of the Jews in their worship. They were not considered equal partners in Judaism, though, and they were not allowed to mingle with the Jews in worship in the temple. In fact, in the second temple, there was a warning sign at the limits of the court of the Gentiles that warned them not to go any farther, under the penalty of death.

The Christian church, however, has been commissioned to go *into* all of the world and make disciples for Jesus. This is impossible to accomplish without intermingling with unbelievers in the world at large. The Great Commission (Matthew 28:19-20) is a commission to go to the world and change it rather than to abandon it.

In His prayer, which follows His farewell discourse, Jesus prays,

I have given them your word and the world has hated them, for they are not of the world any more than I am of the world. My prayer is not that you take them out of the world but that you protect them from the evil one. They are not of the world, even as I am not of it. Sanctify them by the truth; your word is truth. As you sent me into the world, I have sent them into the world. (John 17:14-18, NIV)

There are two truths that we need to see in this passage. First, Jesus prayed that we *not* be removed from the world but that we would be protected from the evil enemy, whose temptations are the real problem that we face when we engage our society. It is not just being in the society around us that causes us to fall. Christians have been "in the world, but not of it" for over two thousand years, with a reasonable degree of success. It is in learning how to do battle with the enemy through the word and the Spirit of God within us that will protect us from succumbing to the temptations that the Prince of this world has to offer.

Second, our separateness comes from our relationship with Jesus Christ and our knowing and following the word of God. This is a spiritual separateness rather than a physical one. Our allegiance to God's word is what sets us apart. The word used in this passage for "sanctify" means "separate."[35] Our separateness comes from our upholding and practicing the truth of the word of God. I heard a preacher recently who said that when he is told that something "will not work in today's society" he reminds the person that we, in fact, are not living in today's society but are living for Christ and according to His ways within modern society. We are to be, literally, a society within society. Paul put it this way:

Don't copy the behavior and customs of this world, but let God transform you into a new person by changing the way you think. Then you will learn to know God's will for you, which is good and pleasing and perfect. (Romans 12:2, NLT)

Additionally, Paul makes it clear that when he talks about not associating with certain persons, he is talking about *believers* who live unrighteous lives and practice things that are contrary to the will of Christ:

> When I wrote to you before, I told you not to associate with people who indulge in sexual sin. But I wasn't talking about unbelievers who indulge in sexual sin, or are greedy, or cheat people, or worship idols. *You would have to leave this world to avoid people like that.*" (1 Corinthians 5:9-10, NLT; emphasis added)

Beware of the "Traps" in the World

Even though we have the power of the Holy Spirit and the knowledge and power of the word of God, the enemy wants to "neutralize" us. There are many "traps" that he has set for us so that, if he can catch us in one of them, he can make us ineffective in our Christian lives. One of these is the "goodness" of worldly morality.

I once got very confused about what it meant to be "in the world." I was confused about the better part of the moral values of the world because they were sometimes close enough to Christian values that it appeared to me that they were the same. After all, this is the same society that has laws against killing and stealing and swindling and even certain types of sexual immorality. Many unbelievers have a very highly developed sense of right and wrong and very much desire to "do the right thing" and to be fair and upright in their dealings with others. It becomes easy for us to believe that we are "on the same page" with our worldly neighbors. It then becomes as easy for us to join the world in doing the wrong thing as it is to join them in doing the right thing.

Often, telling the difference between right and wrong is intuitively obvious, yet on the other hand, many of my Christian friends of days past were very legalistic in their approach to discerning right from wrong. If it wasn't clearly written in the Bible, or in their denomination's public statements, they didn't feel obligated to do it. Often, this approach makes believers less like Jesus and more like the Pharisees.

We can readily see how the world can look at Christians and think that they are just as good and even better than the believers.

We need to get involved in the economic, social, and political process that our society makes available to us. These are the tools that have been provided for us, particularly in a democracy, to have an effect on that society. But it is easy for us to get involved in these processes as an end in themselves, and to forget that our real purpose is to minister to this society in the name of Jesus and according to His word and His standards. Our authority and commission come from Him, and it is to Christ and Christ alone that we owe our primary allegiance.

Peter gives us the following analysis of the difference between the way that the Christians should live in contrast to the society around them and a warning that the secular society will not understand what we do:

> You won't spend the rest of your lives chasing your own desires, but you will be anxious to do the will of God. You have had enough in the past of the evil things that godless people enjoy—their immorality and lust, their feasting and drunkenness and wild parties, and their terrible worship of idols.
> Of course, your former friends are surprised when you no longer plunge into the flood of wild and destructive things they do. So they slander you. (1 Peter 4:2-4, NLT)

Commit Your "Retirement" to God

This book was birthed by my admittedly negative reaction to two statements made in the book *The Purpose Driven Life*. The first of these reads:

> Retirement is not the goal of a surrendered life, because it competes with God for the primary attention of our lives.[36]

And a second statement, very much like the first:

> [An] eternal inheritance, not retirement, is what you should be looking forward to, and working for . . . Retirement is a short-sighted goal.[37]

I retired in 1995, from a twenty-five-year career in law enforcement. Although I have remained gainfully employed since then, I consider myself a retired person. The world and the society around me considers me a retired (or at least, semiretired) person. My primary sources of income are retirement plans.

To say that I have become closer to the Lord in retirement would be a massive understatement! To say that I am an exceptional case would be a massive overstatement. A vast number of my retired friends and acquaintances have not only drawn closer to Christ during their retirements but have found the time for Bible study and prayer and for areas of service and ministry that they previously were unable to do. In our employed lives, we were more often witnesses in the context of our chosen careers. In retirement, we are free to follow the Holy Spirit into any context, without worry about earning a living.

We have been told many times in recent decades that our generation is redefining retirement. No less, those of us who are believers in Jesus Christ can, and should, redefine not only our retirement but what it means to serve our Lord and to be His church within that so-called retirement. I doubt that there is anywhere in our society that this is more true than in the full-time RV lifestyle.

As we discussed earlier, many of our brothers and sisters in the Lord do not understand our desire to do what we do. They seem to have a narrow (and dare I say, unbiblical) view of what the church of Jesus Christ is. They take the words "planted in the house of the Lord" (Psalm 92:13) out of context and use those words to present themselves as superior to us because they are serving God in the same congregation every week. God bless them. I sincerely hope that they are, in fact, serving Him in the way that *He* has chosen for *them* to follow.

But what about us? Are we full-timers sinning by abandoning attendance and service perpetually in the same local congregation? Are we falling from grace, led astray by the siren call of the open road, and being rendered ineffective in our Christian walk? Should we sell our RVs and settle down to a life of Sunday school, morning worship, and Bible study in (and only in) a specific local church? Or is the Lord giving us a different vision? Is he calling us out as He did those early disciples when persecution drove them out from Jerusalem "to the uttermost parts of the earth"? Are we being scattered in our day by the Holy Spirit? Are we called by Him to be "going forth in the Name"?

I was a young man who had found myself in a position of leadership in church when I first remember reading these words from Paul to Timothy:

> Don't let anyone think less of you because you are young. Be an example to all believers in what you say, in the way you live, in your love, your faith, and your purity. (1 Timothy 4:12, NLT)

At that time, this verse had a meaning to me that I suspect was close to the same meaning it had for Timothy in his day, as he was probably no older than I was at the time and faced the same kind of thing that I did. It occurs to me, though, in this stage of life that the principal teaching of this scripture is the same when the idea is reversed and applied to those of us who are older and who have chosen, at God's direction, what we call "retirement" as our lifestyle. So let me paraphrase this passage in a new way:

> Don't let anyone think less of you because you are retired, or because you are a full-time RVer. Be an example to all believers in what you say, in the way you live, in your love, your faith, and your purity.

Wow! When you think about it that way, it really says it all! Be an example to all believers of what they ought to be, whether we are living on the road or not. Commit your retirement to the Lord as you would commit any stage of life to Him. Use the opportunities that it brings, that He brings you. Use it to the fullest. If you have always lived a proper Christian life, continue to live it out in your retirement. If you have wandered away from Him as I had, make it a time to come back and get renewed and reacquainted with the One who loves you and who wants to draw near to you as you draw near to Him.

And so finally, let me admonish you in light of everything we have discussed in these preceding pages to resolve to do all of the following:

- Pray "without ceasing" and at least once every day, have an intimate two-way talk with God.
- Read your Bible (at least one chapter in the New Testament) every day.
- Belong to a church.
- Attend church somewhere every week.
- Be a biblical steward of all that God has entrusted to you.
- Be engaged in ministry as God directs you.
- Grow in grace and knowledge of Jesus Christ.
- Don't let it be a secret that you are a Christian.

If you have never come to Jesus for the first time, I sincerely hope and pray that as you have read the pages of this book, you will have recognized that you need Him and that He loves you and wants you to come to Him and accept His great salvation and the life that He has planned for you from the foundation of the world.

Many people in our world talk about God and believe in God as some kind of cosmic force that is out there somewhere. Many more even go so far as to believe that God is near (yet distant) and that He can answer our prayers when we get in a jam but otherwise leaves us to fend for ourselves. I could go on and on. There are many vague, indefinite ideas about God that are being peddled on us by the "modern" mind, but these are not enough. James wrote,

> You say you have faith, for you believe that there is one God. Good for you! Even the demons believe this, and they tremble in terror. (James 2:19, NLT)

How remarkable! Even the devil and his henchmen believe not just in the existence of a god but the existence of the one true God! The difference is that they are not following Him but have struck out on their own and are going in the opposite direction.

The path that we need to follow to be different from the devil and the forces of evil and to go in the opposite direction away from them is the path that God Himself has set out for us as revealed in His word and in His Son.

> In the past God spoke to our forefathers through the prophets at many times and in various ways, but in these last days he has spoken to us by his Son, whom he appointed heir of all things, and through whom he made the universe. The Son is the radiance of God's glory and the exact representation of his being. (Hebrews 1: 1-3, NIV)

I have always thought that the words expressed here, that Jesus is the "exact representation" of who God is and what is on His mind, and that by following Jesus Christ, we are following God Himself and are indeed following the path that God has set for us in the way that it has pleased Him for us to go. His word expresses that there simply is no other way of salvation.

> Salvation is found in no one else, for there is no other name under heaven given to men by which we must be saved. (Acts 4:12, NIV)

So if you have never accepted God's perfect salvation in Jesus Christ or if you are unsure about whether you have and where you stand with Him, take a moment and settle the matter right now. Believe that He is the Savior and the Son of the living God. Turn and go toward Him rather than away from Him, for that is the meaning of true repentance. Ask Him to come in to your heart and be your Savior.

As I write this, the face of full-time RVing is changing. Gasoline prices have backed off significantly from their all-time highs of either side of four dollars a gallon and are lower now than they have been in years. Yet the fear remains that the price of fuel can skyrocket up again as quickly as it fell. This is bound to have an effect on how many of us stay out on the road and how much actual traveling we do as compared to how long we stay in one spot. Yet the full-time RV community seems to remain intact.

There are plenty of late-model RVs that I see in every campground. People are still buying them and striking out on the road, both as part-timers and full-timers. Those that I meet who are enjoying the full-time RV lifestyle are finding ways of continuing. Very few seem to want to give it up. If anything, the RV community has grown since I joined it.

As I look out my window, I am surrounded by about 240 rigs belonging to folks that I know and work with who are full-timers. Probably all will move from this place when this work season is over. This is, after all, Iowa. Who wants to spend the winter here?

A few years ago, many were driven to become Workampers by stock market reversals that reduced their incomes. Today, many are driven to Workamping by the necessity of higher fuel prices and are getting jobs to pay for the fuel needed to keep them on the road. This is creating new Workamper communities that are making it easier for us to reach folks with the Gospel.

The snowbird communities seem to be remaining intact as well. In August we got one of the last available spots in the popular South Texas park where we will spend the winter. Opportunities abound here as well, as park congregations and Bible study groups flourish in these destination parks.

And then there are all those club-sponsored rallies that many attend. I don't go to these, but I do read the Good Sam *Highways* and the *Escapees* magazines, and it appears that these popular gatherings are more frequent and better attended than ever.

The opportunities to be the church of Jesus Christ to the RV community are many. The Holy Spirit is out here with us on the road in a unique and special way. We have discussed at length what it means to be a Christian full-time RV traveler. Now it is time to put it all into practice.

Go forth in the Name of our Lord, Jesus Christ!

Visit my blog at www.glennrivers.blogspot.com for further reading.

GLENN RIVERS

APPENDIX 1

A Note to My Catholic Friends

I F YOU HAVE already read this book or have at least taken a close look at it, you have probably noticed fairly quickly that it is written from an Evangelical Christian perspective. This is the point of view by which I understand and from which I practice my faith. I have to write about what I know, and these few pages which follow will probably demonstrate to you that I don't really know an awful lot about the Roman Catholic faith.

We Evangelical types have gotten the reputation of being "Catholic bashers," and sometimes it has been deserved. Generally speaking, though, I think we have gotten a "bad rap" on this matter. You Catholic folks should be able to understand this, as you have gotten a few "bad raps" yourselves throughout the years. So let me go on record as saying that I am *not* a Catholic basher.

I grew up in a neighborhood in St. Louis where Catholics outnumbered all others by about three to one. In the public school system that I attended, Catholics had an only slightly smaller majority than in that neighborhood. We really didn't segregate ourselves by religion, so I have always had many Catholic friends. If there was any part in me that harbored the attitude of a Catholic basher, it disappeared once and for all during the twelve years that I worked part-time in a Catholic hospital.

I do not mean to say that I recognize no difference in the way we practice our faith. I do, however, want to convey that I have nothing but respect for the Catholic Church and all that they are doing throughout the world in the name of Jesus Christ.

Second, I wish to give you the impression that, in spite of our differences in the way we practice our faith, this book is for you too and that you can adapt the ideas presented here to your needs and that you too can benefit from reading it.

I read a marvelous book recently titled *The Born-Again Catholic* by one Albert Boudreau, who is himself a devout, practicing Catholic. He talks about many of the same ideas that I do in this book. His basic thesis is that the experience of having a close, personal relationship with God through Jesus Christ and the experience of following the Holy Spirit in daily life has always been a part of the Catholic experience. I suggest that you read his book. It is available through the publisher, iuniverse.com, or through Amazon.com. It has been granted an imprimatur, which term I was not familiar with, but I think that it means that it is approved by the Catholic Church for you folks to read.

His book is not always an easy read, especially in the first few chapters. He quotes several sources so historically diverse as the early Church Fathers to the Vatican II documents to prove his point, as well as such modern Catholic writers as Fr. Brennan Manning and Anne Field, OSB.

I started reading Mr. Boudreau's book long after I started writing *Going Forth in the Name*. In fact, I learned of its existence while I was investigating some prospective publishers. I didn't read his last few chapters until I was nearly finished writing. I was amazed to find how many of our thoughts paralleled each other. In his last chapter, he has written a few paragraphs about some of the subjects about which I have written chapters. Two items in particular are notable. First, he also emphasizes the need to get involved in the personal reading of the scriptures, a subject which I consider to be one of the most important that I have discussed. I have learned through reading Boudreau's book that there is a very good modern Bible translation by Catholic scholars called the "Jerusalem Bible" and its updated version (1998) the "New Jerusalem Bible" I am unfamiliar with this translation myself, but it is my understanding that it is a study Bible that is highly recommended among Catholics.

Second, Mr. Boudreau recommends, on page 193 of his book, that his readers "continually" read Christian books, as I have also recommended for my readers in chapter 8 of this book. He says in addition,

> The Father uses men and women of all denominations, and you shouldn't feel that only Catholic literature is useful. In fact, I've found non-Catholic authors speak clearer and more powerfully than Catholic authors.

It is my sincere hope that you will follow his advice and read *Going Forth in the Name* with Catholic eyes and adapt it to the Catholic mind and practice. All our differences notwithstanding, we should take to heart the words of the apostle Paul:

For there is one body and one Spirit, just as you have been called to one glorious hope for the future. There is one Lord, one faith, one baptism, and one God and Father, who is over all and in all and living through all. (Ephesians 4:4-6, NLT)

Thank you for your attention and may God bless you as you go forth in His Name.

A Daily Bible Reading Plan for Beginners and Rebeginners

THE FOLLOWING PLAN is based on several plans that I have used over the last forty-five years. The very first daily reading plan that I used was one that I found in a Bible that I had been given as a gift when I first became a member of a church and began to get serious about living the Christian life. I mention this only because, to my surprise, this plan did not start at the first page of the New Testament and continue straight through to the last page. Instead, it interspersed the New Testament books so that the four Gospels were read intermittently throughout the year. I liked that arrangement, and I continue to be surprised that most reading plans do not follow such an arrangement.

The arrangement that I have chosen to follow is, first of all, Luke's two-volume account of the history of the Christian church. This is, of course, Luke's Gospel, followed by the book of Acts.

Next, we go to what most scholars regard as the oldest of Paul's letters and, perhaps, the oldest book in the New Testament, the book of Galatians. This is then followed by Paul's earlier letters in what I believe are their approximate chronological order of writing. I chose this arrangement to give the reader a glimpse into the earliest of written Christian thought, since most of these early letters of Paul probably predate the actual writing of the Gospels themselves. Most of them were written at the same time as the events of the book of Acts are occurring.

Next comes the Gospel of Mark. While I have heard convincing arguments for both Gospels of Matthew and Mark as to which was the earliest written, I arbitrarily selected Mark to be next, as it seems to have the preponderance of followers for being the earliest Gospel.

Following Mark's Gospel, I have placed the later letters of Paul.

Next, I have placed the Gospel of Matthew, followed by the General Epistles (those written by writers other than Paul or John).

Finally, I have placed the Gospel of John and the other writings of John, including the Revelation.

The goal is to read one chapter of the New Testament each day. There are, of course, less than 365 chapters in the New Testament (260, to be precise), so that leaves us with plenty of days, after we have finished reading through the entire New Testament. For the remainder of the year, I have selected to reread several books in terms of my opinion as to their importance to us as Christians who are beginning to read the Bible.

It is incorrect to say that any book of the New Testament is any more or less important than another. They all speak to us through the Spirit of God, their Author, as He determines to speak to us at any given time along our journey. That is why daily Bible reading is so important. Yet I feel I should divulge to you my reasons for selecting these.

In Acts and Galatians, we will reiterate what we read earlier about the history of the early church and how God dealt with them.

Romans is a thorough expansion by the apostle Paul of his understanding of the Gospel of Jesus Christ.

Hebrews too is a presentation of the Gospel in terms familiar to the Jewish audience and an argument as to why the way of atonement through Christ is "better" than the old covenant that they had followed for so many centuries.

Ephesians, Philippians, Colossians, Philemon, 1 Timothy, and Titus represent classic advice on how to live the Christian life and how to conduct oneself in the church.

First John, often neglected in Bible study, teaching, and preaching, offers its own unique wisdom that is not to be missed.

Second Timothy, 1 and 2 Peter, and Jude represent what I like to think of as "famous last words" with Paul and Peter at the end of their lives along with Jude, offering advice as to the importance and the necessity of preserving the faith in the perilous times to come.

For the occurrence every four years of the 366th day, I have selected the farewell discourse of Jesus found in John 14-16. I regard this as one of the most important teachings in the New Testament about living the Christian life.

This reading plan is not laid out by specific calendar dates, so it can be started at any time in the year. Ideally, if one were to begin on December 23, you would find yourself reading the Christmas story on Christmas Eve. But don't get overly concerned about when you start. Don't get overly concerned about where you start. Let your concern be that you do, in fact, start and that you see it through to the finish.

Read, listen to His voice, be blessed, enjoy, and grow in the grace and knowledge of our Lord Jesus Christ.

DAILY BIBLE READING CALENDAR

Date	Reading
Day 1	Luke 1
Day 2	Luke 2
Day 3	Luke 3
Day 4	Luke 4
Day 5	Luke 5
Day 6	Luke 6
Day 7	Luke 7
Day 8	Luke 8
Day 9	Luke 9
Day 10	Luke 10
Day 11	Luke 11
Day 12	Luke 12
Day 13	Luke 13
Day 14	Luke 14
Day 15	Luke 15
Day 16	Luke 16
Day 17	Luke 17
Day 18	Luke 18
Day 19	Luke 19
Day 20	Luke 20
Day 21	Luke 21
Day 22	Luke 22
Day 23	Luke 23
Day 24	Luke 24
Day 25	Acts 1
Day 26	Acts 2
Day 27	Acts 3
Day 28	Acts 4
Day 29	Acts 5
Day 30	Acts 6
Day 31	Acts 7
Day 32	Acts 8
Day 33	Acts 9
Day 34	Acts 10
Day 35	Acts 11
Day 36	Acts 12
Day 37	Acts 13
Day 38	Acts 14
Day 39	Acts 15
Day 40	Acts 16
Day 41	Acts 17
Day 42	Acts 18
Day 43	Acts 19
Day 44	Acts 20
Day 45	Acts 21
Day 46	Acts 22
Day 47	Acts 23
Day 48	Acts 24
Day 49	Acts 25
Day 50	Acts 26
Day 51	Acts 27
Day 52	Acts 28
Day 53	Galatians 1
Day 54	Galatians 2
Day 55	Galatians 3
Day 56	Galatians 4
Day 57	Galatians 5
Day 58	Galatians 6
Day 59	1 Thessalonians 1
Day 60	1 Thessalonians 2
Day 61	1 Thessalonians 3
Day 62	1 Thessalonians 4
Day 63	1 Thessalonians 5
Day 64	2 Thessalonians 1
Day 65	2 Thessalonians 2
Day 66	2 Thessalonians 3
Day 67	1 Corinthians 1
Day 68	1 Corinthians 2
Day 69	1 Corinthians 3
Day 70	1 Corinthians 4
Day 71	1 Corinthians 5
Day 72	1 Corinthians 6
Day 73	1 Corinthians 7

Day 74	1 Corinthians 8	Day 113	Mark 2
Day 75	1 Corinthians 9	Day 114	Mark 3
Day 76	1 Corinthians 10	Day 115	Mark 4
Day 77	1 Corinthians 11	Day 116	Mark 5
Day 78	1 Corinthians 12	Day 117	Mark 6
Day 79	1 Corinthians 13	Day 118	Mark 7
Day 80	1 Corinthians 14	Day 119	Mark 8
Day 81	1 Corinthians 15	Day 120	Mark 9
Day 82	1 Corinthians 16	Day 121	Mark 10
Day 83	2 Corinthians 1	Day 122	Mark 11
Day 84	2 Corinthians 2	Day 123	Mark 12
Day 85	2 Corinthians 3	Day 124	Mark 13
Day 86	2 Corinthians 4	Day 125	Mark 14
Day 87	2 Corinthians 5	Day 126	Mark 15
Day 88	2 Corinthians 6	Day 127	Mark 16
Day 89	2 Corinthians 7	Day 128	Ephesians 1
Day 90	2 Corinthians 8	Day 129	Ephesians 2
Day 91	2 Corinthians 9	Day 130	Ephesians 3
Day 92	2 Corinthians 10	Day 131	Ephesians 4
Day 93	2 Corinthians 11	Day 132	Ephesians 5
Day 94	2 Corinthians 12	Day 133	Ephesians 6
Day 95	2 Corinthians 13	Day 134	Philippians 1
Day 96	Romans 1	Day 135	Philippians 2
Day 97	Romans 2	Day 136	Philippians 3
Day 98	Romans 3	Day 137	Philippians 4
Day 99	Romans 4	Day 138	Colossians 1
Day 100	Romans 5	Day 139	Colossians 2
Day 101	Romans 6	Day 140	Colossians 3
Day 102	Romans 7	Day 141	Colossians 4
Day 103	Romans 8	Day 142	1 Timothy 1
Day 104	Romans 9	Day 143	1 Timothy 2
Day 105	Romans 10	Day 144	1 Timothy 3
Day 106	Romans 11	Day 145	1 Timothy 4
Day 107	Romans 12	Day 146	1 Timothy 5
Day 108	Romans 13	Day 147	1 Timothy 6
Day 109	Romans 14	Day 148	2 Timothy 1
Day 110	Romans 15	Day 149	2 Timothy 2
Day 111	Romans 16	Day 150	2 Timothy 3
Day 112	Mark 1	Day 151	2 Timothy 4

Day 152	Titus 1	Day 191	Hebrews 8
Day 153	Titus 2	Day 192	Hebrews 9
Day 154	Titus 3	Day 193	Hebrews 10
Day 155	Philemon	Day 194	Hebrews 11
Day 156	Matthew 1	Day 195	Hebrews 12
Day 157	Matthew 2	Day 196	Hebrews 13
Day 158	Matthew 3	Day 197	James 1
Day 159	Matthew 4	Day 198	James 2
Day 160	Matthew 5	Day 199	James 3
Day 161	Matthew 6	Day 200	James 4
Day 162	Matthew 7	Day 201	James 5
Day 163	Matthew 8	Day 202	1 Peter 1
Day 164	Matthew 9	Day 203	1 Peter 2
Day 165	Matthew 10	Day 204	1 Peter 3
Day 166	Matthew 11	Day 207	1 Peter 4
Day 167	Matthew 12	Day 206	1 Peter 5
Day 168	Matthew 13	Day 207	2 Peter 1
Day 169	Matthew 14	Day 208	2 Peter 2
Day 170	Matthew 15	Day 209	2 Peter 3
Day 171	Matthew 16	Day 210	Jude
Day 172	Matthew 17	Day 211	John 1
Day 173	Matthew 18	Day 212	John 2
Day 174	Matthew 19	Day 213	John 3
Day 175	Matthew 20	Day 214	John 4
Day 176	Matthew 21	Day 215	John 5
Day 177	Matthew 22	Day 216	John 6
Day 178	Matthew 23	Day 217	John 7
Day 179	Matthew 24	Day 218	John 8
Day 180	Matthew 25	Day 219	John 9
Day 181	Matthew 26	Day 220	John 10
Day 182	Matthew 27	Day 221	John 11
Day 183	Matthew 28	Day 222	John 12
Day 184	Hebrews 1	Day 223	John 13
Day 185	Hebrews 2	Day 224	John 14
Day 186	Hebrews 3	Day 225	John 15
Day 187	Hebrews 4	Day 226	John 16
Day 188	Hebrews 5	Day 227	John 17
Day 189	Hebrews 6	Day 228	John 18
Day 190	Hebrews 7	Day 229	John 19

Day 230	John 20		Day 269	Acts 9
Day 231	John 21		Day 270	Acts 10
Day 232	1 John 1		Day 271	Acts 11
Day 233	1 John 2		Day 272	Acts 12
Day 234	1 John 3		Day 273	Acts 13
Day 235	1 John 4		Day 274	Acts 14
Day 236	1 John 5		Day 275	Acts 15
Day 237	2 John		Day 276	Acts 16
Day 238	3 John		Day 277	Acts 17
Day 239	Revelation 1		Day 278	Acts 18
Day 240	Revelation 2		Day 279	Acts 19
Day 241	Revelation 3		Day 280	Acts 20
Day 242	Revelation 4		Day 281	Acts 21
Day 243	Revelation 5		Day 282	Acts 22
Day 244	Revelation 6		Day 283	Acts 23
Day 245	Revelation 7		Day 284	Acts 24
Day 246	Revelation 8		Day 285	Acts 25
Day 247	Revelation 9		Day 286	Acts 26
Day 248	Revelation 10		Day 287	Acts 27
Day 249	Revelation 11		Day 288	Acts 28
Day 250	Revelation 12		Day 289	Galatians 1
Day 251	Revelation 13		Day 290	Galatians 2
Day 252	Revelation 14		Day 291	Galatians 3
Day 253	Revelation 15		Day 292	Galatians 4
Day 254	Revelation 16		Day 293	Galatians 5
Day 255	Revelation 17		Day 294	Galatians 6
Day 256	Revelation 18		Day 295	Romans 1
Day 257	Revelation 19		Day 296	Romans 2
Day 258	Revelation 20		Day 297	Romans 3
Day 259	Revelation 21		Day 298	Romans 4
Day 260	Revelation 22		Day 299	Romans 5
Day 261	Acts 1		Day 300	Romans 6
Day 262	Acts 2		Day 301	Romans 7
Day 263	Acts 3		Day 302	Romans 8
Day 264	Acts 4		Day 303	Romans 9
Day 265	Acts 5		Day 304	Romans 10
Day 266	Acts 6		Day 305	Romans 11
Day 267	Acts 7		Day 306	Romans 12
Day 268	Acts 8		Day 307	Romans 13

Day 308	Romans 14	Day 348	Titus 3
Day 309	Romans 15	Day 349	1 John 1
Day 310	Romans 16	Day 350	1 John 2
Day 311	Hebrews 1	Day 351	1 John 3
Day 312	Hebrews 2	Day 352	1 John 4
Day 313	Hebrews 3	Day 353	1 John 5
Day 314	Hebrews 4	Day 354	2 Timothy 1
Day 315	Hebrews 5	Day 355	2 Timothy 2
Day 316	Hebrews 6	Day 356	2 Timothy 3
Day 317	Hebrews 7	Day 357	1 Peter 1
Day 318	Hebrews 8	Day 358	1 Peter 2
Day 319	Hebrews 9	Day 359	1 Peter 3
Day 320	Hebrews 10	Day 360	1 Peter 4
Day 321	Hebrews 11	Day 361	1 Peter 5
Day 322	Hebrews 12	Day 362	2 Peter 1
Day 323	Hebrews 13	Day 363	2 Peter 2
Day 324	Ephesians 1	Day 364	2 Peter 3
Day 325	Ephesians 2	Day 365	Jude
Day 326	Ephesians 3	Day 366	John 14-16
Day 327	Ephesians 4		
Day 328	Ephesians 5		
Day 329	Ephesians 6		
Day 330	Philippians 1		
Day 331	Philippians 2		
Day 332	Philippians 3		
Day 333	Philippians 4		
Day 334	Colossians 1		
Day 335	Colossians 2		
Day 336	Colossians 3		
Day 337	Colossians 4		
Day 338	Philemon		
Day 339	1 Timothy 1		
Day 340	1 Timothy 2		
Day 341	1 Timothy 3		
Day 342	1 Timothy 4		
Day 343	1 Timothy 5		
Day 345	1 Timothy 6		
Day 346	Titus 1		
Day 347	Titus 2		

NOTES

1. Adventureland is a family-oriented amusement park and resort complex in Altoona, Iowa, a suburb of Des Moines. It consists of the amusement park itself, a hotel, and an RV park. It is the largest single-location employer of Workampers in the United States.

2. The Septuagint, so named because it was reported to have been the work of seventy (or seventy-two) highly esteemed Hebrew scholars, was a translation of the Old Testament from Hebrew into Greek. It was translated between 300 and 100 BC. Copies of it were probably used by Greek-speaking Jews in the Roman Empire. It was the "Bible" that was, in most cases, quoted by Jesus and the apostles.

3. James Strong, "Greek Dictionary," in *Strong's Exhaustive Concordance of the Bible* (Peabody: Hendrickson, *n.d.*), s.v. "paracletos" (word no. 3875).

4. For a more detailed theological discussion of the Holy Spirit and Spiritual gifts, an excellent source is Dr. Wayne Grudem's *Systematic Theology* (Grand Rapids: Zondervan, 1994), especially chapters 51 and 52.

5. Strong, "Greek Dictionary," in *Concordance*, s.v. "ekklesia" (word no. 1577).

6. John H. Leith, *Basic Christian Doctrine* (Louisville: Westminster/John Knox), pp. 235-36.

7. Ibid., p. 239.

8. Ibid.

9. Jill Briscoe, *Here Am I, Lord . . . Send Somebody Else* (Nashville: Thomas Nelson, 2004), p. 15.

10. Wayne Grudem, *Systematic Theology* (Grand Rapids: Zondervan, 1994), pp. 864-65.

11. The late Dr. William L. Muncy, often cited in this book, was the professor of religion under whom I studied at the school which is now known as Missouri Baptist University. Dr. Muncy was a man of keen intellect who also had a talent for being able to simplify the most profound truths of Christian theology. He was known for his sense of humor, his love for our Lord Jesus, and his love of sports.

   Dr. Muncy was a native of Arkansas. He received his bachelor's degree from Ouachita Baptist University in Arkadelphia, Arkansas, and his BD and

ThD from Central Baptist Seminary in Kansas City, Kansas, where he taught for several years following a successful career as a Baptist pastor in several communities, including St. Joseph, Missouri. When the Baptist College was organized in St. Louis, Dr. Muncy laid aside his prestigious position and followed the leadership of the Holy Spirit to become the professor of religion on this fledgling institution. In addition to his teaching position, he was also instrumental in guiding the institution to becoming the prominent institution that it is today.

Dr. Muncy was the Bible personified to those of us who knew him. He knew the entire English Bible by heart (or so I was told) in more than one translation and was intimately familiar with the Greek and Hebrew texts. He preached regularly in many pulpits in the greater St. Louis area. Many people, both clergy and laity alike, have fond memories of him standing before their congregation. When he announced, "Let us stand for the reading of God's word," he would proceed to hold the closed Bible in his hands out in front of him and proceed to recite verbatim and without error (as many who were reading along could attest) the appropriate passages from the 1901 ASV of the Bible.

Given Dr. Muncy's love of athletics, it is not surprising that the gymnasium at Missouri Baptist College is named for him.

Dr. Muncy served as an inspiration to several generations of church leaders of all denominations, both clergy and laity.

The two books written by Dr. Muncy, *A History of Evangelism in the United States* and *Fellowship with God Through Christian Stewardship*, are still available through Amazon.com.

Most of the anecdotes that I cite in this book are taken from my own memory or that of others and may not be entirely accurate, as some forty-plus years have transpired since I last saw the great man.

12. In his *Systematic Theology*, pp. 912-18, Dr. Wayne Grudem makes a good case for the idea that there was, in fact, one specific model of church government in the New Testament, that being a plurality of elders selected by either the apostles or the members of the local church itself. While I am not entirely convinced of the historical factuality of this, I see much virtue in that system itself, particularly as it could counteract abuses of power by making elders accountable both to one another and to the whole congregation.

13. For a complete discussion of the practice of laying on of hands in the New Testament, see Dr. Wayne Grudem's *Systematic Theology*, pp. 959-61.

14. John H. Leith, *Basic Christian Doctrine* (Louisville: Westminster/John Knox, 1993), p. 235.

15. Author unknown, Sunday bulletin of Triumphant Lutheran Church, Bracken, Texas; March 19, 2006, Mark Grubmeyer, pastor.
16. Charles Colson and Ellen Vaughn, *Being the Body* (Nashville: W, 2003), p. 307.
17. These authors also make statements that are derogatory in nature regarding those of us who are not "planted" in the same church always. Colson and Vaughn go so far as to say, "Failure to commit to a particular [local] Church [*sic*] is failure to obey Christ" (p. 307). I strongly disagree with their attitude. In fairness to these authors, however, perhaps they do not know any full-time RVers. As I have pointed out in this book, there has been a notable failure of local churches to reach out to RV parks in ministry.
18. Rick Warren, *The Purpose Driven Life* (Grand Rapids: Zondervan, 2002), p. 136.
19. English language scriptures distributed by the Gideons are in either KJV or NKJV, as there are no royalties attached to these translations. The savings from not having to pay royalties results in the Gideons having several thousand more dollars available to apply to additional scripture distributions.
20. Henry H. Halley, *Halley's Bible Handbook*, 25th ed. (Grand Rapids: Zondervan, 2000), pp. 1077-80.
21. Preface to the New King James Version (Nashville: Thomas Nelson, 1982), p. viii.
22. Eugene H. Peterson, *The Message* (Colorado Springs: NavPress, 2003), p. 8.
23. Dispensationalism is a theological system that began in the nineteenth century with the writings of J. N. Darby. It is generally associated with the doctrine of premillennialism. Among other things, this system teaches that biblical history is divided into seven periods or dispensations. It is from this idea that it gets its name.
24. Phillip D. Yancey, *Prayer: Does It Make Any Difference?* (Grand Rapids: Zondervan, 2006), pp. 101-54.
25. Although the authorship of this book is ascribed to Brother Lawrence, a Carmelite monk, it was actually compiled after Lawrence's death by Abbé Joseph de Beaufort and is made up of de Beaufort's record and recollections of conversations with Brother Lawrence and of several letters that Lawrence had written him.
26. Strong, "Hebrew Dictionary," in *Concordance*, s.v. "yashab" (word no. 3427).
27. As delivered at the Adventureland Chapel, various dates, summer of 2007.
28. Strong, "Greek Dictionary" in *Concordance*. The most commonly used word for "steward" and "stewardship" is "oikonomeo" or variations thereof. See Strong's words no. 3621, 3622, and 3623.
29. W. L. Muncy Jr., *Fellowship with God Through Christian Stewardship* (Kansas: Central Seminary, 1949; repr., Whitefish: Kessinger Publishing, 2005), p. 57.
30. Ibid., pp. 119-20.
31. *Merriam-Webster Dictionary* (New York: Pocket Books, 1974), p. 582.

32. Strong, "Greek Dictionary," in *Concordance*, s.vv. "katallage" (word no. 2643), "katallasso" (no. 2644).

33. Glenn Rivers' blog, "Set It and Forget It Christians," posted March 19, 2007, www.glennrivers.blogspot.com.

34. Colson and Ellen, *Being the Body* (Nashville: W, 2003), pp. 316-17.

35. Strong, "Greek Dictionary" in *Concordance*, s.v. "hagiazo" (word no. 37).

36. Warren, *The Purpose Driven Life*, p. 81.

37. Ibid., pp. 119-20.

SDG

LaVergne, TN USA
14 October 2009
160909LV00004B/8/P